The Diffusion of War

The Diffusion of War

A Study of Opportunity and Willingness

RANDOLPH M. SIVERSON AND HARVEY STARR

Ann Arbor

THE UNIVERSITY OF MICHIGAN PRESS

355.02
562 d

Copyright © by the University of Michigan 1991
All rights reserved
Published in the United States of America by
The University of Michigan Press
Manufactured in the United States of America

1994   1993   1992   1991   4   3   2   1

Library of Congress Cataloging-in-Publication Data

Siverson, Randolph M.
   The diffusion of war : a study of opportunity and willingness /
Randolph M. Siverson and Harvey Starr.
      p.   cm.
   Includes bibliographical references (p.   ) and index.
   ISBN 0-472-10247-8 (alk. paper)
   1. War.   2. International relations.   3. World politics—19th
century.   4. World politics—20th century.   I. Starr, Harvey.
II. Title.
   U21.2.S58   1991
   355.02—dc20   91-17286
                                                          CIP

British Library Cataloguing in Publication Data
Siverson, Randolph M.
   The diffusion of war : a study of opportunity and
   willingness.
   1. War
   I. Title   II. Starr, Harvey
   355.02

   ISBN 0-472-10247-8

Distributed in the United Kingdom and Europe by
Manchester University Press, Oxford Road,
Manchester M13 9PL, UK

To our parents

Preface and Acknowledgments

This book is about the contagion of international war, the most extreme form of conflict among nations. The subject has not received nearly as much attention as has the onset of war. In part this is because so many of the perspectives from which war has been studied approach the subject in a manner that implicitly steers attention away from looking at the onset and expansion of war as related but different parts of the conflict processes. At the outset it is worth considering briefly the variety of perspectives on the study of war and then reflecting on the role of contagion in the process.

Beneath the apparent agreement on some of the basic reasons why war is important and why it is important to study war, there are a variety of perspectives on war, its study, and why that study is crucial to the human condition that have little or nothing in common except an agreement that war is undesirable. Indeed, while war has been and continues to be a central focus (many argue *the* central focus) of the study of international relations, we believe that the following observation, made by Most and Starr (1983, 139) is still true:

> In reading the literature on the causes and consequences of international conflict, one is struck immediately by the fact that scholars appear to share no common understanding of why wars are important to study, what such events represent or indicate, or how to operationalize and measure the very phenomena that so concern them.

There are many specific definitions of war, or lists of the characteristics that make up a war, as related to the concern with operationalization and measurement noted here. More importantly, there have been different conceptions of the *nature* of war across history. These conceptions have had different views of what sort of phenomenon war is, and thus the *meaning* that war has for humans. Given different meanings of this sort, people have sought very different things from studying, analyzing, or simply thinking about war.

In its starkest manifestation, people have looked at war from a "cataclysmic" or a "strategic" perspective (Rapoport 1966). That is, war might be seen in the same way as a natural disaster. As Karl Deutsch (1967, 91) puts it, "War, like famine, plague, hailstorm or earthquake, is seen as an inexorable act of God or nature, an event that comes and will come again. . . . " Related to this, Deutsch also notes that war may be seen as part of an inevitable historical dynamic, or, in a related image, there is a view of war as necessary in the struggle of good against evil, sometimes taking the form of an image of Armageddon, the *last* battle between good and evil.

Alternatively, war may be seen as a strategic act that results from the decisions of humans. The image of war in this case may range from Augustinian and Thomistic images of human weakness to *just war* calculations to wars of last resort that imply a naive rationalism that alternatives to war no longer were available, or an image of war as the failure of control, or war as obsolescent by some form of cost-benefit analysis (see Deutsch 1967 for a full description of these images).

As such images have changed across history and cultures, war has taken on different meanings, and its study has been for different purposes. Under a number of the more rationalistic images, war is conceptualized as a mechanism that redistributes wealth, status, and power. This is the study of war to understand its consequences—what effects war has on the resulting international system in terms of some set of power hierarchies.

Rationalistic images have also promoted a conception that war is a specialized *legal* state of affairs or condition existing among nation-states (see, for example, Wright 1965) and that the purpose of its study is to understand how the incidence and magnitude of war might be reduced through the use of legal mechanisms. A legalistic approach also has led analysts to try to understand war through the study of the units, generally nation-states, that could be involved.

War has other consequences. These are the somatic violence, death, and destruction that result from the clash of arms (e.g., see Galtung 1969). Many observers are concerned with war because it has physical costs in that it generates the death of humans and the destruction of property. Such costs have also sensitized observers to a concern with the moral price of war. Both types of costs must be factored into rationalistic images of war; while both are involved in images of the *just war,* only the latter may be considered in Manichean images of war as a holy struggle between good and evil.

In studying war, the traditional object of study has been the escalation of some conflict to war. Because the predominant modern images of war are primarily rationalistic, especially focusing on the loss of control (as well as the absurd costs generated by a possible nuclear war), contemporary scholars have been concerned with the *process* by which disputes among states escalate into a violent conflict. That is, a prominent perspective on the study of war is the study of the process of social conflict, including the occurrence of stages of conflict, or a conflict dynamic, that escalates through threat and coercion to the use of violence, and finally the large-scale use of violence (see Most and Starr 1983; Rummel 1979, pt. 4).

This conflict-process perspective has many variants, almost all of which are concerned with the *causes of war*. What gets such a process in motion? What promotes or impedes the escalation of the process to violence? What are the characteristics of states (or other groups or even individual actors) involved in this process? What are the relationships between the attributes and/or behavior of state-dyads? How does the state system affect the process of escalation that leads to violence?

The research reported here attempts to go beyond the question of dispute escalation and instead to understand the factors that attract parties to a conflict. Thirty years ago Schattschneider (1960) offered a classic analysis of American politics that was centered on the contagious nature of conflict and how politicians struggle to control the scope of conflict. He began by observing: "Nothing attracts a crowd as quickly as a fight. Nothing is so contagious" (1). The same may be said of many international wars. Our goal is to understand the conditions under which war contagion or the spread of war is most likely to happen.

As with any major research project, we have benefited from the contributions and assistance of others in terms of resources, labor, and scholarship. At the University of California, Davis, we wish to acknowledge with thanks the helpful research assistance of Sherry Lutz, Drew Froliger, Juliann Emmons, and Ellen Morgan in the generation and analysis of the data, and the extraordinarily timely programming assistance of Brenda Gunn. At various stages in the preparation of the manuscript Kathi Miller, Linda Potoski, Roberta Anderson, and Kelly Ramos were indispensable. We also owe a major debt to Alan Olmstead, the director of the Institute for Governmental Affairs at the University of California, Davis; without his support the collection of the data on international borders would not have taken place. At the University of South Carolina, the Institute of International Studies sponsored two colloquia at which various portions of this project were presented and discussed.

Papers related to this project were also presented at the Third World Congress of the Peace Science Society (International) in 1988, the annual meeting of the International Studies Association (1989), the annual meeting of the Western Political Science Association (1989), and the annual meeting of the American Political Science Association (1989). We wish to thank all those panelists and discussants who commented on our work and who stimulated our thinking (and even rethinking) about this project, with special thanks to Walter Isard, John O'Loughlin, and Michael Ward. Earlier versions of chapters 2 and 3 have appeared in the *American Political Science Review* and *Political Geography Quarterly*.

This project could not have moved as rapidly to completion without the formidable encouragement and assistance of Colin Day, director of the University of Michigan Press. The book is now a better one because of the valuable comments of the (once anonymous) referees for the press, Bruce Russett and Melvin Small. We hasten to add, however, that none of the above bears responsibility for any errors that may be present; the authors blame each other for these.

Finally, we need to acknowledge our intellectual debt to a "third author," a friend and colleague who stood always at our shoulder, a tangible intellectual presence if not a physical one: Benjamin A. Most.

Contents

CHAPTER 1

The Identification and Consequences
of the Diffusion of War

One knows where a war begins but one never knows where it ends.
　　　　　　　　　　　　　—Bernhard Von Bülow, 1898

In the summer of 1914 Europe was at peace. There was nothing unusual about this; there had been a long period of relative peace among the major powers of Europe since 1870. To be sure, there had been a few wars that had attracted several nations as participants, mainly minor powers in the Balkans; there had been several arms races that had been seen as extremely dangerous to the peace, particularly the so-called dreadnought race between Great Britain and Germany; and there had been several crises of what were thought to be serious proportions (e.g., Fashoda, Agadir, and Morocco); but, these events had been either contained, resolved, or managed. The only war between major powers was the Russo-Japanese War, and that had been fought far from Europe. While the peace in Europe may have been uneasy at times, it was peace nonetheless.

On June 28, 1914, the assassination of the Archduke Franz Ferdinand and his wife in the small, then-little-known Bosnian town of Sarajevo ignited a crisis between the governments of Serbia and Austria-Hungary. At first the crisis seemed manageable, particularly in view of the Serbian concessions, but then it erupted into a limited war between those two nations. Initially, the war, too, seemed to be a minor affair, but within a week the conflict had spread to encompass seven European nations, including all the major powers except Italy, which was to join later. World War I ultimately grew to involve the serious participation of fifteen states, which collectively lost more than nine million lives (Small and Singer 1982, 89).[1]

If the spread of war shown in World War I was an isolated phenomenon, if it was the only instance of more and more nations being drawn into deadly

---

1. The size of World War I would have increased to 34 states if we included those nations that declared war on at least one of the participants but did not suffer more than 100 battles deaths (Wright 1965, app. 19, table 41).

conflict, then it might not be particularly interesting to note the statement from Prince Von Bülow given at the beginning of this chapter. Unfortunately, while the case of World War I is particularly conspicuous, approximately one-third of the international wars since 1816 have exhibited some degree of diffusion. The converse of this, of course, is that two-thirds of those wars did not spread. What accounts for this variation? Why do some wars, such as World War I, spread while others, such as the Russo-Japanese War (1904–5), do not spread in any remotely similar manner?

There is another related aspect of war diffusion that is of significance. Although many states became involved quickly in the diffusion of what was to become World War I, there was considerable variation in the amount of time that passed before other states joined. After Austria-Hungary and Serbia, the next state to enter the war was Germany, which, through its declaration of war on Russia, became a participant on August 1, 1914, only three days after the initial attack on Serbia; Germany then declared war on France on August 3. The United Kingdom joined the war just four days after that on August 5, 1914. Other nations continued to trickle in, with the final participant, Greece, not joining until June 29, 1917. What accounts for the variation in the length of time it took nations to join ongoing wars?

The research that we report here is aimed at understanding *who* becomes involved in a war and the length of *time* that it takes for involvement to take place. We do this by seeking the answers to two broad theoretical questions. First, can we identify the necessary conditions for war diffusion? That is, can we identify the conditions that seem particularly conducive to a nation's becoming involved in a war between two other nations? Second, can we use the identified conditions to understand the speed with which nations are likely to become involved in a war once it starts?

Taking a diffusion perspective on the study of war forces us to deal explicitly with a number of significant issues. As will be developed to varying degrees throughout this book, these issues include concerns as to what exactly war is; the conception of war as an interdependent outcome of two or more states; the need to focus on conflict processes, especially those of escalation once war has begun; and the crucial issue of the consequences of war for more war within a conflict-process framework. A diffusion approach to war, as an investigation of how and why war grows and spreads, requires the analyst to be concerned with what happens *after* the initial outbreak of any war.

Why Study the Growth of War?

Traditionally, the study of war has almost exclusively been concerned with the subject of initial war outbreak. However, there exists a second dimension, the impact of the war on states other than the original belligerents, an impact that sometimes may lead to the direct involvement of other states in the war. It was not until relatively recently that analysts began to consider wars as the outcome of both processes. While it is true that most wars have only two participants, the deadliest, most costly, and longest wars are accompanied by this process of *diffusion*. The goal of this book is to discuss a set of factors that lead to the activation of this second process, that is, to *how wars grow*.

War, thus, not only produces consequences for the political, military, and economic structure of the postwar system, or consequences in terms of human life and property, but also has strong consequences for the growth (and outbreak) of war itself. Consider the following findings. Starr (1972, 1975) reports on the impact of a state's war coalition experience on the probability of the outbreak of future war (and the participants in such war). The study of war coalitions permitted several observations about the consequences of war for future war. The payoff distribution within war coalitions was discovered to have an impact on the choice of future allies and enemies. Distinct patterns were discovered differentiating dyads of states that were wartime alliance partners from other types of dyads. Wartime partner dyads were much more likely to be allies in future wars and much less likely to be enemies. In addition, the distribution of territorial spoils within victorious war coalitions reflected the level and utility of wartime military contributions. Thus, being a part of the coalition, in many cases *joining* one of the belligerents, provided the opportunity to contribute militarily and benefit from the redistribution of territory. Such territorial redistribution had an effect on the military, strategic, and economic postwar structure and, perhaps more importantly, often provided the cause of future conflict (see particularly Diehl and Goertz 1988; Diehl 1988).

In general, as the number of participants in a war increases, so does the level of death and destruction associated with that war. Inspection of war data such as those produced by the Correlates of War Project (Small and Singer 1982, for example) indicates that in the post-Napoleonic period, the interstate wars with the greatest number of casualties were those that grew to include the largest number of participants. The four wars ranked highest in battle deaths were also ranked the top four in nation months; all four involved infection (see Small and Singer 1982, 102–3, table 5.1).

Similarly, in Richardson's consideration of the statistics of deadly quarrels (1960), the most deadly wars between states were those that had spread to new participants. The only two conflicts falling into his magnitude of death range of $7 \pm 1/2$ are World Wars I and II. Given that Richardson's primary aim was to understand the set of factors that accounted for the death of humans, the relationship between wars that grow in size and the magnitude of death helps to explain why Richardson devoted three of twelve chapters to the question of how best to model the growth of ongoing wars.

While on occasion the addition of new participants might help to bring an ongoing conflict to its conclusion more quickly, (for example, the United States's entry into World War I), again, in general, the addition of new participants has tended to increase the duration of war as well as its deadliness. This is especially true if new participants act to redress the balance of military fortune for the side losing at the time of entry. A prominent post–World War II example is the entry of the People's Republic of China into the Korean War at a crucial juncture for the North Koreans. The increased human costs of the war that followed were clearly related to the increased duration. American and Soviet entry into World War II similarly expanded both the duration and costs of a war that had appeared to be heading for a much more rapid conclusion.

The costs of war are not measured solely in human life. As Paul Kennedy (1987) demonstrates, historically wars have imposed a tremendous economic burden on the states involved (see also Rasler and Thompson 1983). Kennedy demonstrates the economic costs, debt, and mechanisms needed to fund that debt, which in turn have plagued the great powers of the West across history as they have pursued war as a policy option. Consistent with our argument, Kennedy also shows that as a war lasts longer and involves a power fighting in more theaters and against a greater array of opponents, the economic burdens of war increase also; his discussion of the dilemmas facing Spain under the Hapsburgs is particularly relevant: "Enormous though its financial and military resources appeared to contemporaries, there was [sic] never sufficient to meet requirements" (44). The consequence of this was that " . . . Spain resembled a large bear in the pit: more powerful than any of the dogs attacking it, but never able to deal with all its opponents and growing gradually exhausted in the process" (49).

The growth of wars thus may have profound effects on the duration of war and the human and economic costs of war. However, for those students of war concerned with the consequences of war for the political structure of the international system, the effects of increased participation ramify even further. First, the addition of states into wars often has structural consequences. That is, the new partners either have been or become alliance partners (and not simply informal members of a war coalition). The wartime and postwar structure of the international system in regard to military capability, strategic and political relationships is strongly affected by such alliances. We might even speak of alliances affecting a *prewar* structure, if the structure of the newly created international system provides the opportunity or lays the groundwork for the next war.

A second, and clearly related consequence is presented in the extensive literature that has addressed the possibility of "long cycles" in the rise and fall of systemic hegemons (following the work of Modelski 1987; Modelski and Thompson 1989), whether based on military factors, economic factors, or some combination thereof (see Goldstein 1988; Kennedy 1987; *International Studies Quarterly* 1983; Gilpin 1981; Midlarsky 1989). While this literature has developed a variety of models for the explanation of long cycles, or the rise and fall of great powers, many of those models explicitly include the factors that work to weaken a hegemon or dominant power, opening the way for the challenge of some ascendant power or coalition (see Gilpin, for example).

Kennedy's argument clearly indicates that the costs of war impose economic burdens on great powers that account for the weakening of those states and the cyclic rise and fall of states as leaders in the world system. Rasler and Thompson (1983) provide data strongly supporting a similar argument. Indeed, they move from the contention that war leads to larger national debts to argue that *global war* (not just any war between states) is the key source of public debt for great powers. Global wars have been wars that have grown through processes of diffusion or infection. If Rasler and Thompson (and Kennedy) are correct, such wars have created the largest debt for great powers, and such debt is the key ingredient in the decline of such great powers.

While not all wars *grow,* those that do so tend to be longer and more costly and have significant effects on the structure of power in the international system. Thus, if we are concerned with war as a phenomenon that humans can understand and do something about, we are concerned with war because of the consequences it generates in terms of death and destruction; if we are concerned with war in terms of the political, economic, and strategic changes generated in the international system (including the cyclic rise and fall of dominant states), then we must be concerned with the *growth of war* as one form of diffusion and as one consequence of war for war. In short, central to the study of diffusion is the realization that "there are both interesting and important questions to be investigated after war has broken out" (Starr 1975, 6).

The Application of Diffusion Analyses to War

Diffusion is a complex concept with multiple meanings and has been addressed by sociologists and geographers as well as political scientists (see Klingman 1979; Cliff and Ord 1981; Welsh 1984; Most and Starr 1990). Here it should suffice to note that to diffuse means to spread out. Such spreading out may take place through various processes and take a number of different forms. Previous work has been generally within the *diffusion as emulation* tradition. Here the occurrence of some event, war, for example, provides a set of stimuli for emulation, or the occurrence of new war participation by states not originally at war.

In the emulation tradition, outside events or stimuli have been conceived as prototypes that present cues, models, rules of thumb, or analogies to decision makers. Ross and Homer (1976, 5) present an elaboration on this theme, noting that diffusion "may involve such diverse principles as imitation, role modeling, reference-group behavior, relative deprivation, status anxiety, learning, rational evaluation or alternatives based on observation, imposition by force, or the power of new ideas."

In chapter 2 we will develop at length the ways in which the international environment creates the contexts for state decision and behavior. Here we need only briefly note that the existence of war in the system provides cues and prototypes that affect the risks, opportunities, and calculations of decision makers. As war diffuses to new participants, this also has an impact on the decision calculi, or incentive structures, of policymakers.

Thus, for any of a number of possible reasons given by Ross and Homer, the existence of war may affect the proneness of nonbelligerents to enter the war. Previous work on diffusion has involved the effects of war on the participation of states in *new war participation* as well as the possibility of simply joining a war already in progress. Joining ongoing wars, or the process of the growth in the number of belligerents in ongoing wars, has been termed *infection*. Here, the existence of an ongoing war changes the probability that states not at war not only will go to war but will join those conflicts in progress. Houweling and Siccama (1985, 647) note examples of this happening in multilateral wars, such as the Italian attack on Greece in World War II.

Perhaps the most crucial continuing issue in the series of Arab-Israeli wars, for example, has been whether or not any specific conflict would grow to involve other nations. The concern has been with both local joiners and possible nonregional joiners. Thus, while the question of Jordanian participation (its occurrence and timing) was a crucial one in the 1973 Yom Kippur War, new participant escalation in terms of including the superpower sponsors of local belligerents has always been of foremost importance.

Indeed, the post–World War II concern with the escalation of violent conflict, whether regional conventional conflicts or civil war, is really a concern with infectious diffusion. Would one or both superpowers become involved, raising the specter of nuclear exchange? As we will see throughout this book, alliances have been employed (at least in part) as trip wire mechanisms that would *insure* the spread of war to the United States and thus could be used to bolster the credibility of America's deterrent threats. This was particularly true of NATO and the American forces stationed in Central Europe. The role of alliances and military commitments in the infectious diffusion of war is best illustrated by the conversation between British and French military officials in 1910, as reported by Tuchman (1962, 68):

> "What is the smallest British military force that would be of any practical assistance to you?" Wilson asked. Like a rapier flash came Foch's reply, "A single British soldier—and we will see to it that he is killed.

The question of infection or the escalation of ongoing war to new participants is therefore a crucial issue in the study of international politics and foreign policy, even when not explicitly recognized as such. The primary concern of this book is the study of diffusion and the consequences of war for war. It will focus on diffusion as infection and the processes by which ongoing wars spread. The agents or conduits or mechanisms by which diffusion takes place will be investigated through the opportunity and willingness framework and the interaction opportunity model it generates. The interaction opportunity model, in turn, is based on how ongoing war (the prototypes sending out stimuli such as cues) affects the incentive structures of decision makers to join existing war. We will now review several different approaches to the study of war diffusion, thus providing a context for the interaction opportunity model within the relevant diffusion research literature.

A considerable amount of the early empirical research on war attempted to explain its onset by looking at the effects of one or several independent variables on a dependent indicator variable, such as, for example, the nation months of war (Singer and Small 1968; Singer, Bremer, and Stuckey 1972) or the number of nations at war (Singer and Small 1974). The initially unrecognized problem with this procedure is the conflation of the onset of war (a dichotomous variable) with the size of a war (a continuous variable). The problem, however, has consequences significantly beyond what type of measurement is appropriate, since by using the size of a war (while the theory under investigation specifies that onset is being measured), the distinct possibility of diffusion is neglected. Put differently, what is overlooked is the possibility that the process by which the first two nations in a war *begin* fighting may be considerably different from the process by which the war spreads as other nations become involved. This blurred distinction neglects what is usually referred to as Galton's problem, a topic to which we will return shortly. The important point is that under circumstances in which diffusion is present but unrecognized, the resulting models are necessarily misspecified and most probably investigated with inappropriate methods.

Following the recognition of this problem, recent research has moved in two new directions. One of these focuses on the behavior of the initial participants in wars and attempts to explain only their behavior. Generally this is accomplished by considering the onset of war as the end product of the escalation of a dispute between nations (Bueno de Mesquita 1981; Bueno de Mesquita and Lalman 1986; Leng and Gochman 1982; Maoz 1982; Siverson and Tennefoss 1984). The second line of research, based upon the recognition of the problem outlined above, is that wars might diffuse or be contagious through a process of infection. That is, the occurrence of an event, in this case war, on the part of two nations will increase the probability that other nations will engage in that same behavior. In general, research on the possible diffusion of war began with the question of determining the extent to which wars were in fact infectious (Davis, Duncan, and Siverson 1978; Most and Starr 1980; Faber, Houweling, and Siccama 1984) and, after establishing that they were, then sought to uncover the factors responsible for *variation* in the diffusion processes. In general, two lines of investigation have been followed in seeking to uncover the agents of war diffusion. The first of these is based upon *borders* as interaction opportunities (Most and Starr 1980; O'Loughlin 1984; Ward and Kirby 1987). The second centers upon *alliances* between or among states as indicators of groups of states that share roughly the same international policies and may be willing to fight together for them (Altfeld and Bueno de Mesquita 1979; Siverson and King 1980).

The research presented in this book brings borders and alliances together within a theoretical framework *based* upon the ideas of *opportunity* and *willingness*. The use of this framework permits us to examine ongoing wars as events that alter the incentive-constraint structures perceived by foreign policy decision makers, thus increasing the chances that nations will become involved in an ongoing war. The analyses presented here will be conceived in terms of a research design in which particular conditions or sets of conditions are treatments that may or may not produce effects. In accomplishing this the data set has been expanded significantly in scope and complexity over previous collections, new analytic tools have been added, and greater attention is given to interaction of method, theory, and empirical findings.

Identifying the Process of Diffusion

In the late nineteenth century, Galton (in Taylor 1889) pointed out that phenomena tend to diffuse from one locale to another. As recounted by Naroll (1965, 428–29):

> Galton raised his problem at the meeting of the Royal Anthropological Institute in 1889 when Taylor read his pioneer paper introducing the cross-cultural survey method. Taylor showed correlations ("adhesions" he called them) between certain traits; in the discussion which followed, Galton pointed out that traits often spread by diffusion—by borrowing or migration. Since this is often so, how many independent trials of his correlations did Taylor have?

Following Galton, a number of social scientists have attempted to test for the existence of diffusion effects on different phenomena and to assess their explanatory value. For example, researchers have studied the diffusion of race riots (Spillerman 1970), coups d'etat (Midlarsky 1970; Li and Thompson 1975), alliance formation (Job 1976; Siverson and Duncan 1976), and so on.

The earliest explicit suggestion in the empirical literature that warfare might diffuse was made by Richardson (1960, chaps. 10–12). Richardson attempted to construct a mathematical model that would adequately account for the number of nations on each side of a war. The assumptions that made up Richardson's best fitting model were essentially that the number of nations on each side in a war was the outcome of a process heavily influenced by *geography* and modified by *infection*.

It is likely, however, that because of the technical limitations faced by Richardson, he understated the extent to which wars were enlarged by the process he had identified. Since his models were complex and his computational aids primitive (at least by today's standards), Richardson did not include in his analysis those wars in which there was a total of more than four participants. This excluded seventeen of the ninety-one wars (18.6 percent) in his original data base. Since the seventeen excluded wars are precisely those that would be expected to reveal the greatest amount of infection, it is highly probable that the actual underlying process is more than slightly modified by infectiousness.

Although Richardson's book reporting these findings was published in 1960, it was not until more than fifteen years later that several investigators began looking at the problem of infection again.[2] Zinnes (1976a) and Wilkinson (1980) both reviewed extensively the contributions of Richardson to the study of war, including a recognition of his work on infection, but this was largely incidental to their more general reviews.

More recently, inquiry into the possibility of war diffusion has become a central focus of research. The investigations have thus moved considerably beyond Richardson's data and methods. The use of other data sets on war has permitted the exploration of the extent to which the process of diffusion is general across different conceptions and measures of warfare. Moreover, better methodologies have allowed the more recent research to demonstrate that apparent infection can be produced by any one of several processes, and that some of these are noninfectious in character.

The first question is through what process does war appear to spread? As we have noted, there are several ways to conceptualize diffusion. Different conceptualizations lead to and derive from different models of the diffusion process (see O'Loughlin 1986). We will begin, as did Richardson, with those

---

2. Richardson's research was done prior to World War II in a number of articles. It was not until 1960, however, that the articles were drawn together in a book.

models most closely concerned with infection, as the growth of an ongoing war. In one interesting study, Yamamoto and Bremer (1980) use three probability models to assess the tendencies of major powers to enter ongoing wars. This is an important problem since most major power participation in war takes place as a nation joins an ongoing war. Moreover, it is those wars with major power participants that are usually considered to be the most severe, since those nations, almost by definition, have the greatest capacity to inflict damage upon others.

The three models Yamamoto and Bremer explored are (1) independent choice, (2) one-way conditional choice, and (3) two-way conditional choice. Substantively, these abstract probability models have very different implications. Under independent choice each of the major powers is assumed to have the "same constant probability of entering any particular war, and its probability is not affected by whether or not other major powers enter the war . . . " (201). Under one-way conditional choice, a major power's probability of entering a war will either be held constant or be increased by the entry of another major power. More specifically, one-way conditional choice leads to either no change or an increase in the probability of a major power's entering a war; it cannot lead to a decrease in the probability of that event. Finally, in the situation of two-way conditional choice, the model provides for a major power's probability of entering a war either increasing or decreasing depending upon the choices of other major powers.

> Or, to draw the distinction in a somewhat different way, under two-way conditional choice, the decision of the first power leads to an increase in the probability that the second power will select the same option, regardless of the option chosen, but with a one-way conditional choice process this emulation effect occurs only if the first power decides to enter the war. (203)

When the data on actual major power war entries between 1815 and 1965 are compared to the theoretical distributions generated by the three models, the two-way conditional choice model fits the data much better than the other two fit. Further examination of the major power record of war entry by Yamamoto and Bremer indicates that the fit of the two-way conditional choice model is stronger in the twentieth century than in the nineteenth century. They also note that although the two-way conditional choice model fits the data well, the Polya distribution that results from it can also be arrived at from assumptions of heterogeneity. That is, the same distribution of data implied by the model can result from assumptions that major powers have probabilities of war entry that differ from nation to nation and time to time. Such a process could be the result of nations that become, so to speak, war prone. Thus, although Yamamoto and Bremer demonstrate that major powers apparently influence each other in their propensities to enter ongoing wars, because of the limitations inherent in the models they used to approach the research there remain questions of considerable import. First, is the process of diffusion they observed composed of behavior that is infectious, heterogeneous, or possibly even something else? Second, is possible diffusion limited to the major powers? Both of these questions have, in fact, been the subject of other research that has been relatively successful in answering them.[3]

The identification of the process through which war has diffused has been the object of inquiry by Davis, Duncan, and Siverson (1978) and Most and Starr (1980). Like the report of Yamamoto and Bremer, these two sets of investigators were interested in exploring the processes through which national war participation increased; however, these studies were significantly different from each other in terms of data and methods. We will begin with the latter.

Most and Starr (1976) sought first to distinguish which of several war diffusion processes was operating and second to evaluate the extent to which a particular factor contributed to the process they identified. We will discuss the first aspect of this research here and return to the second in the next chapter. Most and Starr drew upon three data sets on war, a considerably broader data base than any of the other research. First, they used not only the wars between 1946 and 1965 identified by Singer and Small but also a combination of data from earlier war lists of Wright and Richardson compiled and presented by Singer and Small (1972, 82–128) and finally a list presented by the Stockholm International Peace Research Institute, or SIPRI, (1970, 365–73, table 4A.1).

At the outset, Most and Starr (1976) applied what may be termed the traditional approach to the detection of the interdependence of wars, through the comparison of their observed distributions with theoretical distributions generated by the Poisson and modified Poisson models (Coleman 1964, chap. 10). Such a starting point appears appropriate because one of the key assumptions of the Poisson model is that the occurrence of an event does not alter the probability of a subsequent occurrence, while under the assumptions of the modified Poisson the occurrence of an event does alter the likelihood of subsequent events. Hence, it would appear that if the distribution derived from the standard Poisson model yielded the better of the two fits with the empirical distribution, then there was at least preliminary evidence to support the null hypothesis of no diffusion.

The application of the Poisson model to the three different data sets on

---

3. Note also that Houweling and Siccama (1985) used an "epidemiological model" to demonstrate diffusion and that wars were not independent events.

war produces some interesting results. The null hypothesis in each test was the proposition that the observed distribution of wars was Poisson or randomly distributed; the alternative to this was simply that the wars were not random. In the case of the Correlates of War (COW) data, the null hypothesis of random distribution could not be rejected except at the .70 level of significance; at the other extreme, the SIPRI data enabled rejection of the null hypothesis at the .02 level. In the case of the Wright-Richardson data, the results were marginal with rejection being possible only at the .10 level. These findings lead Most and Starr to argue that those different types of war tend to result in different diffusion effects. Put more specifically, it seems reasonable to surmise that international wars involving major powers may not have tended toward diffusion during the 1945–65 period, as much as civil, guerrilla, and colonial wars.

Most and Starr, however, note that three aspects of the traditional Poisson or modified Poisson model make it less than satisfactory in studying war diffusion at any level of conflict.[4] First, it is insensitive to the fact that the number of independent states in the international system increased from 66 in 1946 to 125 in 1965. So as not to conflate their results, they initially limited their analysis to the behavior of the 59 nations that were present throughout the 1945–65 period. Hence any diffusion on the part of the *new* states was omitted.

Second, they note that the traditional approach is insensitive to distinctions among the following: (1) *positive reinforcement,* in which a nation's war participation at t increases the probability of participation at $t + 1$; (2) *negative reinforcement,* the reverse of the previous process; (3) *positive spatial diffusion,* in which the occurrence of a new war participation by a nation increases the probability that other nations will experience war participation; and (4) *negative spatial diffusion,* in which, of course, the occurrence of a new war participation by a nation decreases the probability that other nations will become involved in subsequent wars.

These four types of processes are, of course, fundamentally different, but as Most and Starr demonstrate, they have frequently been difficult to distinguish in aggregated data. However, analysts must be able to make such distinctions if the study of diffusion is to be successful. Presumably, positive and negative processes ought to be distinguishable. Yet, Most and Starr show

---

4. These arguments were expanded in Most and Starr (1981, 2–4), where eight limitations on the Poisson model were discussed. Tests based on the Poisson model may be inconclusive, may be misleading, are unable to distinguish positive spatial diffusion from negative diffusion, are unable to distinguish between positive diffusion and positive reinforcement, are insensitive to changes in the number of potential "initiators" and "recipients," assume similar probabilities across a global sample, yield few insights into the substantive nature of diffusion effects, and fail to suggest how diffusion processes might operate.

that as their data are aggregated into increasingly long periods of time, the Beta term in the modified Poisson model (which may be interpreted as a measure of the degree of diffusion in the events) also increases. The Beta term is a function of the *ratio* between the variance and the mean, and for the data utilized by Most and Starr both of these increase as the time periods of the data are lengthened. However, even if one believes that this difficulty can be overcome, there remains another problem. If a positive Beta is obtained, no means exists to determine whether it was caused by positive spatial diffusion or positive reinforcement. The same is true in the case of a negative Beta.

At least one conclusion with an interesting implication can be drawn from the critiques presented so far. By differentiating among types of diffusion processes, we see that there can be very different sources of war diffusion. The existence of these different underlying processes argues strongly against the use of highly aggregated global models or analyses that are inherent in the application of the Poisson, a point to which we will return. Because all four processes *could* be at work, and because we can find examples to indicate that all four probably are at work, the effects of each could wash out the others at the level of a global analysis. A similar effect is at work in global cross-national studies of the relationship between domestic and foreign conflict (Starr and Most 1985; Stohl 1980).

However, the tendency of this research design to treat all conflicts as being relevant to all nations led Most and Starr to pursue the question of the agent for the spread of war. Most and Starr (1980) argue that one should not reasonably expect war to diffuse throughout the international system as a whole, but rather such diffusion will be constrained within sets of nations that interact significantly with each other.

The work of Davis, Duncan, and Siverson (1978) takes a different combination of approaches to the study of diffusion. Using the Singer and Small data set of all war participants between 1815 and 1965 (not just major powers), they examine the distribution of new warring dyads each year and compare this to the theoretical distributions derived from several substantively distinct probability models. The first is the Poisson, reflecting randomness in the emergence of warring dyads. A second model (Poisson with time varying rate per dyad) could detect heterogeneity over time. A third model (the negative binomial) could detect either heterogeneity over individual nations or addictive contagion. These last two processes are identical except that under addictive contagion each dyad's initiation rate is not constant but, rather, tends to increase with each war. Finally, a model is developed to identify infectious contagion, a process in which a war within any dyad increases the probability that other warring dyads will form. The point of difference between this model and the others is that under it the dyads are not independent in their behavior.

Although the initial match of the data to the models reveals that the negative binomial fits best, the fit is very poor. A test of the model of infectious contagion that *abandons* the independence condition produces a reasonably good fit. Further analyses lead to the conclusion that wars between 1815 and 1965 grew in size through a process of infectious contagion; that is, one dyad's fighting increased the chances of other dyads beginning to fight. Another way of summarizing these results is to say that variation in war is (1) not random, (2) not due to particular periods being more war prone, and (3) not due to particular dyads fighting a great deal (e.g., France-Germany).

An Epidemiological Perspective

Before going any further, we must make a basic point concerning the relative *rarity* both of war and the diffusion of war. Although war may seem to be ubiquitous (it *is* in terms of having some war somewhere taking place), in reality it can be and has been conceptualized as a rare event. When one looks at war in terms of the statistical opportunities that exist for its occurrence, the actual number of times that such an event takes place is remarkably small. There are a variety of ways to measure this phenomenon. For example, Small and Singer (1982, 118–22, table 6.1) provide data on the number of nation months of war taking place in the international system for each year, 1816–1980. This measure is the sum of all months at war for all states at war during any year. Small and Singer then indicate the "percentage of nation months exhausted" in any year given the amount of war that occurred. For example, for a hypothetical twenty state system, there is a total of 240 possible nation months of war for any single year (twenty × 12 months). If during a single year only one war, which lasted four months and had three participants, took place, the total nation months of war for that year would be 12. Since 12 is 5 percent of 240, for that year the percentage of nation months exhausted would be 5 percent.

For the international system, as operationalized by the COW Project, there were 20 years during the 1816–1980 period when *zero* percent of total available war months were exhausted (no war occurred); in an additional 79 years, 5 percent or less of the available nation months of war occurred. That is, in 99 out of 164 years only 0 percent to 5 percent of the available nation months of war were exhausted. As would be expected, the largest percentage of nation months exhausted occurred during the two world wars; the high points during this historical period occurred in 1917 (33.7 percent exhausted) and in 1943 (28.6 percent exhausted). While substantial, this still indicates that even at the height of the two world wars only one-third or less of all the available nation months of war were expended.

From another perspective, Most and Starr (1989, 137) note that in 1980 there were nine interstate or extrasystemic wars underway (using COW data), involving 14 participating states. These figures should be matched against the statistical possibilities that existed. With approximately 155 states in the system, there were 23,870 possible directed (or asymmetric dyads) "and hence statistical opportunities (in the Richardsonian sense) for dyadic war."

Directing their attention to the assertions that either balanced or imbalanced dyads of states (in terms of power) predispose the dyad going to war, Most and Starr found that only .4 percent (four tenths of one percent) of imbalanced dyads between 1946 and 1980 took advantage of that opportunity; only .26 percent of balanced dyads did so (1989, 140).

Whatever list of wars one uses (see Singer and Small 1972, chap. 5; Levy 1983; Most and Starr 1983), the actual number of wars is never very large. Levy (1983, 88–91), for example, lists 119 great power wars for the period 1495 to 1973 (or approximately .25 of a war a year). This rarity of occurrence is responsible for the almost standard use of the Poisson distribution—which is a rare event distribution—for the study of war diffusion.

Using a logical analysis based on opportunity and willingness, Most and Starr (1989, 71–84) develop a conceptualization of war that helps to explain why it is a rarity. Of the sixteen paths that are required by the necessary conditions of opportunity and willingness for a dyad to have a war, only *one* will eventuate in war. Thus, despite the fact that wars have appeared continuously across history and generate highly important consequences, they must be recognized as relatively rare occurrences.

At the same time, as we will see, the diffusion or growth of war is also relatively rare. In the 3,746 nation years comprising the data set we will employ in this research, there were only 94 cases of war diffusion. The overall rate of diffusion, then, is only 2.5 percent. There are thus a great many more opportunities for diffusion in the form of infection than are taken advantage of by states. Key questions to be addressed in this study are these: *Which* opportunities lead to diffusion? Under *what* conditions?

We find ourselves faced with the analysis of the growth of war—a significant question given the consequences that are generated by war—yet we are also faced with a set of relatively rare or infrequently occurring phenomena. This rarity has played a powerful role not only in the methodological choices we have made but in the use of an epidemiological perspective to our overall approach to the study of war and diffusion.

This influence is apparent from our use of the terms *infection* or *contagion* in dealing with the diffusion of international conflict.[5] The analogy is

---

5. In a recent literature review Diehl (1988) also comments on the analogy between the spread of war and the spread of disease in the war diffusion literature. See also the approach taken by Houweling and Siccama (1985) in their "The Epidemiology of War, 1816–1980."

broader than that, however. If the basic concept of contagion is based upon some form of emulation, or the picking up of some form of stimuli that promotes a condition that didn't already exist in some entity, then diffusion is closely related to what Anatol Rapoport (1960, chap. 3) has called "psychological epidemics." Drawing upon our understanding of organic epidemics, he notes (51): "in an organic epidemic, the infected and infectious individual transmits the disease to a number of others, who, in turn transmit it. The transmission is 'nonconservative,' that is, the giver of the disease is not thereby deprived of it."

Not only is there an analogy between diffusion of phenomena such as war and disease, but others have drawn an analogy between the study of war and disease. Such an epidemiological metaphor is central to the work of Francis Beer (1981), with an opening chapter simply titled, "Epidemiology." Beer (4) indicates the important use of the epidemiological metaphor, noting that the comparisons of war to disease and peace to health have appeared in work by individuals such as Sorokin (1937), Richardson (1960), Boulding (1962), Singer and Small (1972), and Alcock (1972). Beer's work is based on two fundamental assumptions: "(1) war is like a disease, for example cancer or heart disease; and (2) we can develop a scientific knowledge of war, similar to the knowledge we have about disease, that will allow us better to describe, predict, and control it." Johan Galtung (1985) has similarly argued the parallel between peace research and medical science, pointing out that each has a normative bias (preferring health or peace over disease or war) and that each requires research, education, and action (although professors of medicine are more likely to be practitioners than professors of international relations).

Norman Alcock brought both aspects of the epidemiological perspective to bear in a 1972 book called *The War Disease* (a book that, in retrospect, deserved much greater attention). Not simply a review of the then-extant empirical literature on war, Alcock developed a "two-phase theory of war" (chap. 13). This theory was based on a set of factors that he argued increased insecurity and hostility and resulted in arms races; these arms races, in turn created conditions during a cycle of arms growth and decline that promoted war at certain points on that cycle.

For our purposes, and the notion that there are states *ready* to catch the war disease, it is important to note Alcock's further argument (207): "Due to war *somewhere* in an arms race system, the natural cycle of arms spending is maintained; moreover *under the stimulus* of these shooting wars, the level of arms spending steadily increases" (emphasis added). It should be clear that in this context, although war is a rare event, *only a little war* in the system is needed for Alcock's model (or similar models) to work.

Alcock did not, however, specify the mechanisms by which states not at war would or could catch the disease. It is here that our concern with what wars cause, the growth of war, and the general question of diffusion becomes important. From an epidemiological perspective diffusion is *key*—it provides a way of thinking about the processes by which states not at war catch the disease; a way of thinking about how war may be infectious or spread through contagion of some sort from states at war to states at peace. Most and Starr (1980, 933) make this point in a straightforward manner: "The general war diffusion hypothesis concerns the possibility that the occurrence of one new war participation will alter the probability of subsequent occurrences."

We have previously investigated two factors hypothesized to be crucial to the working of a diffusion process: borders and alliances. In previous studies, as well as in this volume, both factors have been conceived of as experimental *treatments*—conditions under which the relatively rare phenomenon of diffusion becomes more likely. This is a significant continuation of the epidemiological metaphor, signifying the design of *historical experiments* in lieu of the experiments of medical researchers seeking to identify the treatments that make disease more likely and/or serve to prevent or cure disease.

In the analyses presented here we will be concerned with those states initially at peace at any time t_0, (that is, those countries that were *healthy*). Our various designs are then crafted in such a way as to determine the impact of being *exposed* to the war disease by either or both *treatments* at t_0—having a bordering nation at war (having a "warring border nation," or WBN), and/or having an alliance partner that was at war (having a warring alliance partner, or WAP). The effects of such treatments are investigated by looking at the war participation behavior of the treated states at some t_{+k}.

In part because of the rarity of the diffusion phenomena, those results are not analyzed exclusively in the standard terms of explained variance. In light of the diffusion models that we will present, we have set out a series of expectations of how states should behave, of what the world should look like under certain conditions, and match the resulting behavior of states undergoing treatments to those expectations. We also compare the behavior of the treated states to those countries *not exposed* to WBN or WAP treatments.

The issue of exposure raises the question of limiting factors to the spread of some phenomenon such as disease or war. Without such factors an epidemic—or a war—would continue to grow indefinitely (we will return to this issue at the conclusion of chap. 4). Rapoport (1960, 51–52) discusses a set of limiting conditions, which includes "immunity conferred by the disease itself" (indicating why we are careful to look only at those states currently at peace) and measures to limit "contact among the members of the exposed population."

This latter point would include the existence or use of mechanisms that would limit exposure to some phenomenon. Analogues to this idea can be found in the diffusion literature. The geographer Peter Gould (1969, 11–23), for example, discusses the concept of "barriers" to diffusion, which act to absorb, reflect, or otherwise act to block the wave-like spread of some phenomenon as it diffuses. This directs us back to the consideration of opportunity and willingness as necessary conditions for diffusion. By providing both possibilities and constraints, opportunity and willingness can also be conceived as barriers or limiting conditions to diffusion as well.

The epidemiological perspective thus contributes to the development and understanding of the methodology employed in the research reported here. We have sought factors that are necessary (not sufficient) in the growth of wars. We place our analyses within a framework of *loose necessity* which, we argue, can provide important conclusions without claiming sufficiency (see chap. 2; Siverson and Starr 1989). These factors are used not so much to explain the variance in a "join–no join" dichotomous dependent variable or to predict the occurrence of infrequent events but to indicate how the probability of behavior is altered by our treatments. Skjelsbaek has similarly used an epidemiological metaphor to interpret results on the relationship between international organization (IGO) membership and war:

> The probability of a pair of nations becoming involved in war may be compared to the probability of persons getting lung cancer. In *absolute* terms both probabilities are very low. However, if a person smokes cigarettes, and a pair of nations substantially reduces its number of shared IGO memberships, the probabilities of getting lung cancer and fighting on opposite sides in a war, respectively, are *relatively* much higher than they would otherwise have been. (1971, 59)[6]

The Book to Follow

In this introduction we have tried to indicate the role that diffusion plays in the study of war. The great majority of works on war have been concerned with the causes of war, or, more specifically, with how wars start. We have, in line with our past research interests, indicated that scholars should also be concerned with the consequences of war—what wars cause, how war leads to more war, and more specifically *how wars grow* once they start.

We have also indicated briefly why such growth is important and that the addition of states to ongoing wars can usefully be addressed through the application of diffusion concepts. We have reviewed various diffusion studies in order to provide a context for the diffusion analyses to follow. We have also

---

6. See Bueno de Mesquita (1984, 354–55) for another discussion of rare events, necessary conditions, and the analogy of research on lung cancer in the section "Are My Necessary Conditions Trivial? The Case for Lung Cancer."

introduced one important component of the conceptual context for our analyses—the epidemiological metaphor. The rest of the conceptual framework necessary for understanding these analyses will be presented in the next chapter.

Thus, in chapter 2 we will present the broad intellectual context within which this research has been conducted, introducing the theoretical apparatus of the *opportunity and willingness* framework (see Starr 1978a; Most and Starr 1989, chap. 2). This framework will be used as the backdrop for discussing geo-political phenomena, particularly the manner in which geography and alliances interact, and the way in which each affects the choice situation the decision makers of a state confront in its foreign policy after a war begins.

Having delineated our approaches to the study of diffusion by outlining an opportunity and willingness framework, its derivative interaction opportunity model, and how they may be used to study alliances and the infectious growth of war, we will have presented a full rationale for the research designs executed in chapters 3 and 4. Chapter 3 begins with a description of the data employed, the manner in which they were gathered, and a detailed discussion of research design. An appendix following the final chapter lists the data in an easily accessible form.

The main purpose of chapter 3 is to address the correspondence between opportunity and willingness and the diffusion of war, for all states—major powers and minor—over the period 1816–1965. The impact of borders and alliances on the growth of ongoing wars, individually and in combination, is fully demonstrated to have an important effect on diffusion.

In chapter 4 we change our focus from the diffusion of war across space to exploring the impact of opportunity and willingness on the *time* that it takes new war participants to join an ongoing war. By analyzing the extent to which states entering a war do so at different times, we seek to understand the factors contributing to time variance in joining war.

Chapter 5 will summarize our results but more importantly also serves to draw the analysis together and integrate the findings reported with the international relations literature on war. A final section of this chapter will bring together our conclusions with other aspects of international relations theory.

CHAPTER 2

The Context of Diffusion: Opportunity, Willingness, and Geography

The main purpose of this chapter is to introduce and explain the ideas of opportunity and willingness. Together these form the conceptual context within which we study the phenomenon of diffusion, and the relationships among geography, alliance, and the growth of war. In addition, a second purpose, borrowed from Most and Starr (1989), is the concern with placing empirical research within broader conceptual or theoretical contexts in order to give *meaning* to the concepts being operationalized and the empirical results produced.

Explicating Conceptual Contexts

International relations specialists have traditionally debated the location of the sources of international phenomena such as conflict and cooperation. Some have argued that they rest at the *microlevel,* in the hearts, minds, and calculations of the decision makers of states (e.g., Bueno de Mesquita 1981). Analysts adopting this perspective have focused on leaders' perceptions, decision makers' role-playing behaviors, organizational processes, political bargaining or competition among key leaders and advisers, rational or expected utility calculations, and so on. In doing so, such scholars have suggested that it is the *willingness* of key foreign policy decision makers that precipitates a state's involvement in international conflict.

Theorizing rather differently, other scholars have argued that conflict derives primarily from *macro-*, systemic, or dyadic level processes (e.g., Waltz 1979). Focusing on structural concerns such as systemic polarity, system size, and/or the balance or imbalance of power between potentially opposing pairs of states, these scholars have maintained that an understanding of international conflict cannot be derived from a microlevel or so-called reductionist perspective. They maintain instead that the nature of the system and the character of the dyad give rise to international conflict because such factors create or preclude the *opportunity* for conflict initiation (e.g., Siverson and Sullivan 1983).

While the micro- and macrolevel approaches to international conflict are generally posed as rival or competing explanations, the development of the opportunity and willingness concepts was specifically designed to indicate how the two levels could be integrated or synthesized. Most and Starr (1989), utilizing a series of logical demonstrations, analyses of real world empirical data, as well as computer simulation, demonstrate that the two levels of analysis are indeed complementary. Neither micro- nor macrolevel approaches are individually sufficient for understanding international politics; instead they appear to be jointly necessary.

The Importance of Conceptual Context: Alliances

Despite the many contributions that have been made in the study of international alliances, the research on this topic is one of the best examples of the cited "need to reconceptualize *exactly what* it is that [analysts] want to study, and *why*" (Most and Starr 1984, 392, emphasis in original). Briefly, Most and Starr present a detailed framework for foreign policy substitutability, which argues that varying conditions might lead foreign policy decision makers to *substitute* one foreign policy tool for another. This means that, in a foreign policy situation, *apparently* distinct or incommensurable behaviors could be chosen. Given the situation, or context, there may be a many-to-one mapping, or a one-to-many mapping of foreign policy factors and foreign policy responses. Most and Starr also present and elaborate the notion of domain-specific "nice" laws, a notion that calls for a re-evaluation of the utility of searching only for the broadest general laws. Their argument is that situational, context-oriented "nice" laws that do well for a specific subset of cases are an important goal of research.

These two arguments lead to the conclusion that many international relations phenomena have been studied in isolation, as middle-range ad hoc hypotheses, and have lost their connection to the broader concepts that are actually of concern: "Students of international relations have, in many cases, actually reified the operational indicators of international interaction. We have studied war *qua* war, alliances *qua* alliances, and have tended to overlook the broader international processes and phenomena that such specific forms of behavior represent" (Most and Starr 1984, 392).

If we are to place diffusion in its proper context, then geopolitical considerations are required, and both the study of diffusion and geopolitics embrace important components for alliances. One of the main purposes of this chapter is drawing out systematically the links between alliances and geopolitics. Most research on alliance does not explicitly or systematically take geopolitics into account; similarly, much of the work on geopolitics does not explicitly or systematically deal with alliances (for an exception, see Sloan

1988). Indeed, within the broader concern for cumulation of international relations theory and findings, the lack of cumulation in the study of alliances has come in for specific comment (e.g., see Ward 1982; Job 1981). Alliances need to be reconceptualized in terms of what they *really* represent for particular research questions, of what larger concepts they are examples. Given that foreign policy mechanisms or behavior can substitute for one another, we need to step back and ask what alliances are *about* before we design research to study them or use them as indicators in our studies.

Opportunity/Willingness and Geopolitical Perspectives

One possibly important perspective on alliances, and one that we will argue captures many of the questions that supposedly concern students of alliance, is *geopolitics*. Alliances can take on meaning by thinking of them within geopolitics as part of a broader environmental or *ecological* context. In this respect we have found the work of Harold and Margaret Sprout (1956, 1965, 1969) a particularly useful representation through its stress on the relationship between context and behavior, emphasizing environmental possibility against environmental determinism.[1]

Alliances can be seen as an important component of the Sprouts' "ecological triad" that consists of an entity, an environment, and the entity-environment relationship between them. As we will show, the ideas of the Sprouts were conceptually rich. However, at the same time, when the ideas were developed they were relatively lacking in the empirical specificity necessary for utilization in empirical research. In an effort to overcome this, Starr (1978a) developed the ideas of "opportunity" and "willingness." If we are concerned with how alliances affect the structure of the international environment as well as the calculations made by foreign policy actors within that environment, we are thus concerned with how alliances affect and reflect the opportunity and willingness of states.

In an effort to eliminate the then-prevalent deterministic views of geopolitics, the Sprouts proposed several alternative entity-environment relationships. "Environmental possibilism" holds that the environment presents a configuration of physical possibilities available to entities, possibilities from

---

1. See O'Loughlin and Anselin (1990) or Fox (1985, 31) for a fuller characterization of the Sprouts as possibilists. Fox also elaborates on the Sprouts' role in the development of geopolitical thinking in international studies (27): "Harold and Margaret Sprout are the American political scientists with the most sustained interest in and influence on geopolitical thinking from the 1930's to the 1970's." While not the only possible perspective on geopolitics, nor from the only scholars to present that perspective, the Sprouts' version of possibilism has held an important place in the study of international relations.

which they can make policy choices. Geographical constraint, for example, can be seen as one form of the limits on the "physical possibilities" of humans and the "physical environment" as conceptualized by Giddens (1984, 174ff).

This form of possibilism comprises one component of Starr's idea of opportunity. In brief, opportunity has been developed to mean the possibilities that are available to any entity within any environment, representing the total set of environmental constraints and possibilities. The central use of opportunity in the diffusion studies of Most and Starr has been as an indicator of the degree of interaction (i.e., the use by Most and Starr [1980] of borders as interaction opportunities in the diffusion of violent conflict). As in the Sprouts' environmental possibilism, this simply means that some activity must be physically or technologically or intellectually possible; once the obstacle of possibility is crossed, however, opportunity is, in fact, a continuous phenomenon in which some states have more or less of it with respect to other countries.

Hence, there is a dual nature to opportunity or possibility (especially as it relates to capabilities) that must be recognized. Initially, some capability— technology, ideology or religion, form of government, manner of organizing people to some task, etc.—must be created so as to become part of the range of possibilities available to at least some of the members of the international system. The second dimension to opportunity or possibility is the *distribution* of such capabilities. At one level, all international actors share the same menu of possibilities: Once nuclear weapons are introduced, they become part of the environment that all states have to deal with; the same effect accompanied the creation of the United Nations. At another level international actors may have very different menus of possibilities; for example, the wealth, technological talent, and resources needed to take advantage of the nuclear possibility are not evenly distributed among nations in the system.

Thus, alliances can be seen as part of the international system's structure of possibilities or constraints. Additionally, alliances might also be seen as the means by which states deal or cope with the physical possibilities or constraints presented by geography. To Giddens (1984, 169) structure is "always both enabling *and* constraining" (emphasis added). Alliances, as international structures, have both effects.

The Sprouts also discuss "environmental probabilism," the idea that the structure of possibilities create what we may call an incentive structure that makes some of those possibilities more or less likely. As long as there are possibilities there is room for choice. Although some choices will be more likely than others, the basic notion is that choice is based on probability calculations. Alliances as part of the configuration of environmental structures thus also affect the decision calculi of policymakers. Alliances can be seen as important components of the incentive structures available for states. They are relevant to the choices to be made by decision makers by affecting the perceptions of decision makers as to how costly or risky certain options appear to be.

Alliances comprise, in part, the structure of risks and opportunities that confront decision makers. The perception of these risks and opportunities is covered by the Sprouts' idea of "cognitive behaviorism." This form of entity-environment relationship asserts that the environment affects policymakers only as it is *perceived* by them; these are the images that comprise the decision makers' "psycho-milieu"[2] as contrasted with their "operational milieu" (Sprout and Sprout 1965, 28–30). The Sprouts, of course, are not alone in their emphasis of the importance of the manner in which decisionmakers perceive the world. An extremely large body of literature on the decision-making–perceptions nexus exists in the field of international relations. The importance of the Sprouts' contribution is the explicit linkage between perceptions and the other components of their theory.

Within their scheme the possibilities presented by an environmental context must be perceived, and through this perception, different probabilities are given to different policy positions or choices. It is through the latter process that the Sprouts' idea of cognitive behaviorism is related to willingness—the probability of policy choices reflecting decision makers' willingness to select some possible alternatives over others. The concept of willingness is, therefore, somewhat more familiar to us than opportunity, since it is central to the study of decision making and choice. The dynamics of choice are embedded in a decision maker's image of the world or definition of the situation. Choice is related to a decision maker's calculations of advantage or disadvantage, of cost and benefit. It is through willingness that decision makers *recognize* opportunities and then translate those opportunities into alternatives that, in some manner, are weighed.

Related to our introductory comments, the Sprouts' concepts of environmental possibilism, environmental probabilism, and cognitive behaviorism *require* the combination of both structure-environment and choice-decision process which are captured in opportunity and willingness, respectively. As we have implied, there are complex linkages between opportunity and willingness. They do not create mutually exclusive categories. Anything that affects the structural possibilities of the environment(s) within which decision makers must act also affects the incentive structures for those decision makers. Opportunity and willingness thus become more than organizing concepts. They take on theoretical characteristics when we understand that they describe the conditions that are necessary for the occurrence of events.

Alliances as part of the international incentive structure, thus, may affect

---

2. This brief reference to the psycho-milieu only begins to touch on the "complexity" of "the relationship between place and image" as noted by Kirby (1988, 244).

the willingness of decision makers in their foreign policy choices. But the decision to enter into an alliance itself reflects a willingness to accept the potential costs of alliance as balanced against potential gains.[3] Alliances may be seen as conscious choices of decision makers that indicate positions of policy preference. The formal commitments indicated by alliances demonstrate a willingness to align policy with certain states rather than others; they indicate a willingness to side with some states rather than others. The value of this observation is confirmed by a policy that sought to avoid such commitments—the active policy of affirming a *nonaligned* or neutralist position (especially in relation to United States–sponsored alliances) by Third World states since the 1950s. This willingness to extend a state's commitments also feeds back and becomes part of the total set of incentive structures that each state must work within. In this way alliances reflect the complex relationship between opportunity and willingness.

As noted, the purpose of this chapter is to present a reconceptualization of alliances as a factor related to both opportunity and willingness within a broader geopolitical view of international relations. The explicit development of such a context is required for us to develop, focus, and ground an empirical study of alliances, diffusion, and international conflict.

To achieve this purpose, we will first outline some of the central components of a geopolitical perspective and how alliances might fit within such a perspective. We will then expand on the relationship between alliances and the concept of opportunity within such a perspective and follow with a section on alliances and willingness.

The Place of Alliances in Geopolitics

In a useful review of several recent major treatments of the topic of geopolitics, Osterud (1988) notes the heterogeneous usage of the term and the variety of meanings it has taken on, most of which are either ideological or highly deterministic.[4] He then asserts: "'Geopolitics' is not a term for the general

---

3. While we will briefly review some of the reasons states enter into alliances, it should be clear that this is not the purpose of our discussion (see instead work such as Holsti, Hopmann, and Sullivan 1973; or Starr 1978b). The following discussion linking alliances and geopolitics simply illuminates the range of geopolitical concerns relevant to the strategic or security dimension of alliances.

4. In part, Osterud (1988, 198–99) concludes: "Geopolitical analysis is a manifold phenomenon, ranging on scales from reductionist and determinist 'theory' to awareness of the geographical factor in strategy, and from highly politicized partisanship to a fairly non-committed mode of analysis. Some versions have promoted a very explicit ideological message, with a rather heavy load of pseudo-scientific dross. The geopolitical tradition generally has carried dim ideas, with a diffuse conception of the causal strings between geography, technology and politics. Those varieties of geopolitics lending themselves to the easiest defence have been limited to a more heuristic and illustrative ambition."

linkage of politics to geography. It should rather be understood as a conceptual and terminological tradition in the study of the political and strategic relevance of geography" (191). To make geopolitics more useful, Osterud suggests that it be viewed as the effects of space, topography, position, and climate on political behavior.

It should be clear here that we are concerned with the spatial or topographical orientation linking geography, alliances and international relations.[5] Space and topography are reflected in Harold Sprout's (1963, 192) assertion that all geopolitical hypotheses "represent assessments of opportunities and limitations implicit in the milieux of the interacting nations." He also claims that all such hypotheses fit into either of two categories: "(1) those derived mainly (though never exclusively) from the layout and configuration of lands and seas, or from regional variations of climate, or from the uneven distribution of minerals and other earth materials; and (2) those derived from the distribution of people, or from some set of social institutions or other behavioral patterns."

Some students of geopolitics have taken this basic position and placed it within a highly Realist view of international politics. Cohen (1963, 24), for example, notes that "the essence of geopolitical analysis is the relation of international power to the geopolitical setting." Cohen's definitions of geopolitics all ultimately return to the question of "power" and its distribution in international politics. Sloan (1988, viii) uses almost exactly the same words in noting that "geopolitical analysis as a branch of International Relations attempts to relate international political power to its geographical setting." Sloan goes on to note that geopolitical theory connects geography and political history and is a theory of "spatial relationships and historical causation." As alliances are clearly related to the aggregation of (one's own) or denial of (one's opponents') military capability, and the distribution of policy preferences, we cannot escape the inclusion of realist conceptions to the alliance-geopolitics linkage.

Geopolitics and Context

A more inclusive linkage between geopolitics and alliances is to be found in recent papers by geographers concerned with the manner in which geography creates a *context* for politics. Some geographers have taken to discussing a "new political geography" (see, for example, O'Loughlin and van der Wusten 1986) that has formed around the Sprouts' (1965) ecological model of the entity-environment nexus. Both O'Loughlin (1986, 1987) and Kirby (Kirby

---

5. While we are not concerned with all possible connections between geography and political phenomena, we could propose that alliances broadly relate to both the "functional organization of space" and the "formal organization of space" as developed by Berry (1969).

and Ward 1987; Kirby 1986) have stressed the relationship between geography and international relations in terms of context.[6] O'Loughlin (1987, 2) sees one potential contribution of political geography as "the accurate identification and mapping of the meaningful contexts for the actors engaged in interstate relations." It is clear that these "meaningful" contexts hark back to the Sprouts' "ecological triad" in that they not only include those that immediately surround states but "will vary from the substate through hemispheric to global scales." By taking its cues from the Sprouts, the new political geography is emphatic in its rejection of determinist variants of geopolitics. By asserting that geography matters—through spatial effects and through context, including elements such as territory, borders, and distance—this approach to geopolitics moves away from exaggeration (determinism) but also ensures that geography will not be ignored (Anselin and O'Loughlin 1989). This approach to geopolitics may be captured by O'Loughlin and Anselin (1990) when they note that "geography does not have a subject matter but a perspective. . . . "

In an ongoing research project Anselin and O'Loughlin (see 1989; O'Loughlin and Anselin 1991) have further developed the idea of "spatiality" in their definition of context for international relations. Their conception of spatial analysis contains two elements—location and interaction.[7] They translate the former into the idea of "spatial heterogeneity" and the latter into "spatial dependence."

Spatial dependence captures the phenomena that others (e.g., Most and Starr 1990) have called positive spatial diffusion; it is the *neighbor effect* whereby conditions in neighboring states have an effect on contiguous areas. This is (following O'Loughlin 1986, 1987) spatiality in terms of "first order" effects. But as O'Loughlin (1986) has argued, spatiality should be investigated for second and even third order effects. The idea of spatial heterogeneity captures this broader view, by looking for a *regional* effect—by studying geopolitical spatiality in terms of a regional context.[8] Note that such an

---

6. Kirby (1986, 190) notes: "The logical conclusion from this train of thought is that sociology, not political science, is the obvious model from which political geography should develop its ideas. . . . The core of my statement is that sociology deals with contexts, and has in consequence proved to be fairly successful in examining the logic of social action."

7. They also draw from the work of Hagerstrand (1967), which sets out six aspects of an "epistemological" geographical framework: Events have spatial elements; events have temporal elements; events have a specific character; there is a place where the event is located at both the beginning and end of the time interval; and there are paths of movement or influence.

8. Anselin and O'Loughlin have found these concepts useful in analyzing the spatiality of conflict and cooperation in the African regional context. See O'Loughlin (1986, 1987), O'Loughlin and Anselin (1990), and Anselin and O'Loughlin (1989). Based on these concepts, their continuing research project seeks to distinguish between spatial dependence and spatial heterogeneity, to look at conflict and cooperation as space-time diffusion and as systemic phenomena.

approach—defining spatial context through both neighbor and regional effects—is also consistent with the Most and Starr arguments for "nice laws."

The growth of wars in the Middle East has often exemplified both types of effects. The 1973 war began on October 6, with three contiguous belligerents: Israel, Egypt, and Syria. A fourth original belligerent, Iraq, was not contiguous with Israel but did share a land border with Syria. More regional considerations came into play on October 10, when two additional states joined the war—Jordan, contiguous with Israel; and Saudi Arabia, not contiguous with Israel except across water but contiguous with its Arab League allies, Jordan and Iraq.

These types of discussions by geographers are important in that they indicate the need to incorporate geographical-geopolitical elements into the broader notions of context that have been developed and employed across the social sciences. In a recent paper Goertz (1989, 4–5) reviews how context has been employed. He is critical of the practice whereby "some higher level factor, such as system structure, is viewed to 'cause' some lower level nation-state behavior, such as interstate war." We have specifically used the Sprouts as an example of geopolitical approaches that consciously reject any form of contextual determinism.

Our general notion of context begins with the formal "contentless" characterization of the concept employed by Goertz (1989, 3). By thinking of environments and the entities within them, and how those entities perceive the environment, we are not locked into any specific factor (such as geography) or level of analysis, thus partially avoiding the false micro-macro distinction Giddens (1984, 139–44) warns against. The work of Most and Starr leads us to a conception of context analogous to Giddens' concept of "locale" (1984, 118): "Locales refer to the use of space to provide the settings of interaction, the settings of interaction in turn being essential to specifying its contextuality" (this is also clearly reflected in the work of Anselin and O'Loughlin). The ecological triad of the Sprouts and Starr's opportunity-willingness framework both reflect this concern for the settings of interaction, behavior, and choice.[9]

Additionally, we return to the ideas of substitutability and nice laws by recognizing that context is situationally differentiated and dynamic. Goertz forcefully presents a similar position (1989, 5):

> The fundamental characteristic of contextual indicators is that they are attentive to the shifting meaning of a concept in different environments

---

9. For a full discussion of the concept of interaction opportunity as it was developed for the study of the diffusion of international conflict, see Most and Starr (1980); Starr and Most (1983); and Most, Starr, and Siverson (1989). Sloan (1988, 76) makes a similar argument regarding the manner in which "geographical configurations condition the choices being made by policy-makers."

and thereby generate more valid indicators for general concepts. Likewise, we speak of a contextual theory where the relationship between variables is not just additive, but where the importance of effects of the different variables are theorized to be different in different environments.

Context is not static. Even in our concern with geography as one component of the international geopolitical context, the mapping *process* is to be seen as a dynamic in which space is a contingent factor, where territoriality is constantly in motion. Diehl and Goertz (1988), for example, have identified 775 territorial changes between 1816 and 1980 involving at least one member of the international system (as defined by the Correlates of War Project). These territorial changes, involving any gain or loss of a territory, were clearly associated with international conflict, both before and after the changes. By illustration, the Six Day War (1967), which resulted in Israel's annexation of territory from Egypt, Syria, and Jordan, radically changed the geopolitical context of the Middle East; these changes reverberate even to this day.

From another perspective, Starr and Most (1976) demonstrate that the fifty-nine new states entering the international system between 1946 and 1965 generated 372 new borders of all types, more than doubling the number of borders that existed in 1946. In fact, contiguous homeland borders in the international system rose from 166 in 1946 to 412 in 1965.

By recognizing that context is not static, that territory, actors, and borders change, and that the environment must be perceived to affect choice, we can avoid the idiographic reification of specific places or spaces. Put simply, there is a constant dynamic in the configuration and reconfiguration of space within the context of international relations.[10]

Alliances and Context

Within the geographic component of the environment's structure of constraints and possibilities, alliances have an important role to play in the geopolitical dynamic. As consciously manipulable indicators of policy preference, they can and do change and in so doing change the spatial relationships among friends and opponents: how close they might be; how their relative military capabilities stand in relationship to one another (especially in terms of the decay of the utility of military capabilities across space as conceptualized by Boulding's [1962] loss-of-strength gradient); or, how alliances might "substitute" for borders by altering the configurations of interaction opportunities (see Starr and Most 1976).

---

10. The discussion of the use of logical approaches to the analysis of international relations in Most and Starr (1989) is clear in taking geopolitical aspects of the international system and

Many contextual aspects of geopolitics, including the constraints of "time-space convergence," in Hagerstrand's (1967) terms, can be applied to alliances and their effects on international relations. This can be shown by looking at Harold Sprout's two groups of geopolitical hypotheses (1963). The first looks at the physical constraints of geography (as do Osterud's factors of topography and space [1988]). One theme, to be developed in the next section, concerns the ability of alliances to leapfrog distance and topography and thus affect the willingness of decision makers to risk the costs of alliances.

Sprout's second group of hypotheses is concerned with the social and political configurations of humans in space (what Osterud calls "position"). From a realist point of view, this is exactly what alliances are about when we think in terms of alliances and the balance of power. But the Sprout-Osterud idea is much broader. Alliances *change* the political configuration of the international system. They alter, often quite rapidly and unexpectedly, the politically relevant boundaries; they give new meaning to the political boundaries that are drawn on maps. Alliances thus become central to the *geopolitical* distribution of political preferences, coalitions, and calculations in the international system.

If the international relations scholar is concerned with mapping the spatial and geopolitical contexts within which decision makers must calculate and make choices—the overall constraints and incentive structures provided by opportunity and how they affect the willingness to make policy choices—that scholar must take alliances into account. This is particularly true if we are concerned with the process by which that context is formed and changed. Colin Gray (1977, 1), paraphrasing Spykman (1938), has asserted: "Geography is the most fundamental factor in the foreign policy of states because it is the most permanent." While it is undeniably true that a nation's homeland is relatively permanent, our discussion suggests that Gray's assertion tells only part of the story and captures only part of Spykman's analysis. Geography is important not just because of its relative stability but also because of its role in shaping the dynamics of opportunities and risks.

Through cognitive behaviorism, geography affects the changing perceptions of the possibilities and probabilities provided by the geographical environment. While geography (e.g., in terms of topography or the actual distance between two points) is relatively stable, political changes, such as those brought about by the creation or dissolution of alliances, alter the impact of geography on interaction opportunity and the structure of incentives and risks. To be sure, the physical features may be permanent, but their *meaning*

---

environment beyond the notion of static structure and in demonstrating that there is an important dynamic in the interactions between entities and the geopolitical environment. This point is elaborated in Starr (1987).

to decision makers and to analysts of international relations can and does change dramatically.[11]

The Interaction Opportunity Model

We have noted and stressed the geopolitical role that alliances may play by being an important component of the geopolitical structure of the international system—that alliances change the structural possibilities that exist in the system and that are presented to the actors within that system. Alliances also change the interaction opportunities available to states. Alliances thus are central to the geopolitical structure that constrains states but simultaneously act as mechanisms by which that geopolitical structure and its incentive structures might be changed.

In brief, the geopolitical notion of interaction opportunity was developed by Most and Starr to study the positive spatial diffusion of war. As reviewed in chapter 1, Most and Starr sought to determine which of four possible processes was primarily responsible for the diffusion of war (positive reinforcement, negative reinforcement, positive spatial diffusion, or negative spatial diffusion), and to develop methodologies that would permit the delineation and testing of these processes.

Initial analyses indicated the limitations of stochastic models in their ability both to detect diffusion and to distinguish among the four processes. Based on earlier analyses of borders and war (Starr and Most 1978) they decided to use a model of interaction opportunities, with proximity measured by border contiguity. This model became the theoretical and methodological focus for the study of positive spatial diffusion. Borders were conceptualized and investigated as "constraints on the interaction opportunities of nations." Six categories of borders were developed (Starr and Most 1976) that went beyond the usual conception of border as a contiguous land boundary. Not only water borders were included but also the borders created by colonial territories (which appear to be especially important for major powers).

It needs to be emphasized that within this framework it is reasoned not that borders *cause* wars but rather that they contribute to both the amount of interaction and the probability of various types of interaction (such as war). Drawing upon: (a) what O'Loughlin and Anselin (1990) have called the First Law of Geography, that all places are related to each other but that near places are more related (see Tobler 1979); (b) Zipf's (1949) "principle of least effort," which argues that there will be more interaction between entities that are close than between those that are widely separated; and (c) Boulding's

---

11. Sloan (1988, 215) observes that one of the "tenets" of classical geopolitics was that "the political meaning of geography was in a constant process of change, primarily due to changes in the levels of transport and weapons technology." Sloan exemplifies the stress on technology; we argue elsewhere that similar arguments could and should be extended to alliances.

(1962) variant on both of these formulations, the loss-of-strength gradient—Most and Starr used borders to indicate a proximity between states that increases both the salience of neighboring areas and, in general, the ease of interaction.[12]

It was argued that the more borders a state has, then the greater the number of risks and opportunities it will confront, the greater the likelihood that the state (or its territories) will be only "conditionally viable" in Boulding's (1962) terms, and the greater the level of that state's uncertainty. More importantly, Starr and Most argue that once a war starts on a state's border, that state may find its environment changed in such a way that it participates in a war that it did not intend to join, or it forgoes fighting a war that it had intended to fight.

It is important to note that this conception of interaction opportunity is much broader, and more abstract, than simple notions of borders and warring border nations. Its application to war diffusion is based on the argument that the diffusion of wars is likely to be dependent on the *degree of interaction* that exists between the warring states and the potential participants in new, or ongoing, wars. To the extent that a war is being waged by states with no close ties to other states, we would not expect war to alter the probability of the war behavior of nonbelligerent states.

A second important point to note is that Starr and Most postulate that interaction is a *necessary* (but explicitly not sufficient) condition for the diffusion of wars. They argue that even if international conflicts do diffuse, there is no reason to expect that all states will eventually become involved simply because some first war has already occurred. While spatial diffusion will not operate at a global level, since all states do not have high levels of interaction with one another, the hypothesis is that it will work within *subsets* of actors that are somehow linked together. This conception of interaction opportunity is clearly related to the idea of "nice laws" and permits the investigation of relevant subsets of interacting states.

Alliances as Interaction Opportunities

We have already alluded to the ways in which alliances might also be described in terms of interaction opportunities, but in review:

> The conceptual linkage between borders and alliances is easily delineated. While a nation's borders are not readily manipulable by policy makers, its alliances are. It may be reasonable, therefore to interpret

---

12. This principle has been supported in other empirical research such as Diehl's study of geographic location and contiguity and the escalation of great power confrontation to war (1985, 1206–7): "In summary, if a dispute is contiguous by land to one of the participants, the likelihood

alliance formations (and dissolutions) as attempts by policy makers to alter their border-related risks and opportunities—or, in other words, as efforts to "create" or "destroy" borders. When two contiguous nations ally in a mutual defense pact, for example, they may in a sense be "removing" (or at least decreasing the importance of) their common border. Alternatively, as a nation loses the real borders it once possessed through its colonial possessions, it may have attempted to retain its access and control and legitimize its activity in various regions by creating pseudo- or alliance-related "borders." In that sense, military and economic alliances may have substituted for colonial empires in the post–World War II period. (Starr and Most 1976, 611)

While borders can be conceptualized as an agent of diffusion representing the effects of opportunity, alliances may be used as an agent of interaction opportunity that represents willingness. It is clear that states not only have high levels of interaction with bordering states but also have high levels of interaction with alliance partners. Numerous observers of alliances in international relations have commented on their entangling nature.[13]

Empirical research (Siverson and King 1979, 1980) has explored the extent to which the independent effects of alliance memberships and attributes of different types of alliances account for the extent and character of war diffusion. From the point of view of willingness, these studies, as well as this book, conceive of alliances as a conscious *choice* among foreign policy behaviors or positions. The willingness to form alliances, and alliances with specific partners, may be seen as an indicator of shared policy preference. Put simply, two (or *n*) states forming an alliance are indicating, to some degree, that they share policy preferences. This conception of alliances, which was implicit in the work of Siverson and King, is explicitly developed in Bueno de Mesquita's (1981) model of expected utility; an approach centered on the calculations that lead to willingness.[14]

If alliances can be used to indicate the salience and importance of states to one another and delineate subgroups of highly interacting states, then they

---

of escalation is increased (and increased even more if both sides are contiguous to the site). On the other hand, the absence of contiguity virtually assures that escalation to war will not occur." Diehl goes on to link his results with the concept of opportunity employed here.

13. Those who have described alliances as entangling include Thomas Jefferson and a host of noted academic observers. However, the best formal treatment of alliances that explicitly includes limitations on autonomy as a consequence of alliance is Morrow (forthcoming).

14. Alliances, of course, are not a perfect indicator of willingness. For example, while there is a general tendency for alliances to be reliable, it is clear that reliability is less than complete (Sabrosky 1980). In short, we do not construe alliances as indicating a general willingness to fight. However, alliances have long been recognized as the key means that states have chosen to indicate their political position in the international system.

should have an impact on the diffusion of war similar to that found by Most and Starr using borders as agents of diffusion. This is exactly the research question that will be addressed in the following chapters.

Alliances and Opportunity

The ideas of opportunity and interaction opportunity presented here have primarily derived from the authors' research programs. However, the analysis of alliance as an aspect of opportunity should and can be expanded to cover a variety of alliance studies. If one reason that states form alliances is to *project capabilities*, as well as aggregate capabilities (Starr 1978b), then alliances are involved in the extension of a state's ability to interact militarily with other actors.

This conception of alliances is thus closely related to the idea of the loss-of-strength gradient. If states are concerned with security and military viability vis-à-vis other states as part of their total environmental context, they must be concerned with the physical ability (possibility) of other states to bring military capabilities to bear upon them. One crucial ingredient of such calculations is geographic: What distance must such military capability cross, and what physical barriers stand in its way? The formation of alliances to project capability is thus one mechanism by which states *may overcome* the geopolitical constraints of distance and topographical features. The ring of alliances that the United States built around the Soviet Union during the height of the cold war, most notably NATO, is a straightforward example of this.

Walt (1985) also deals indirectly with alliances as mechanisms to extend the military interaction opportunities of states. His discussion of alternative models that would explain why states join great power alliances is based, in part, on the level of threat that states face. In essence, Walt's argument is that states ally with others on the basis of threat and not power. He indicates four factors that affect the level of threat (9): (1) aggregate power; (2) proximity; (3) offensive capability; and (4) offensive intentions. Clearly, when alliances are formed, they affect the proximity that nations have to one another, as they create new borders and new geopolitical realities. American reaction to Soviet formal agreements in the post–World War II era indicates the possible relationship of alliances, or even informal coalitions, to the perception of threat: either to oneself, as with the Soviet-Cuban relationship, or to third parties in extended deterrence relationships, as in the Soviet agreements with India and the threat to Pakistan, an American client.

States that were once distant are brought closer to each other through alliance commitments; states brought into proximity become more threatened through the projection of offensive capability. By combining Walt's second and third factors, alliances increase the threat to outside parties bordering the alliance partners and do so by overcoming distance and physical barriers, by creating new geopolitical realities. As Walt notes (1985, 10–11), proximate threats can generate either checkerboard effects (under a balancing response) or a sphere of influence effect (under a bandwagoning response). Either way, the use of alliances to project capability creates a threat that reconfigures the geopolitical distribution of power and political allegiance. These effects conform to realist perspectives on geopolitics.

If we look closely at proximity creating threat, we see the phenomenon of states (usually major powers) in a dynamic of expanding their defensive or offensive spheres (aggregating military capability, projecting military capability, or attempting to forestall the opponent from doing either). The interaction opportunities created by new alliance networks as well as alliance-generated borders provide the opportunities for formerly distant states to be proximate, hence to interact, and thus raise the probability of conflictual interaction. This, for example, was exactly one of the functions of American troops in Berlin, where they had been too few and too vulnerable to be anything other than a trip wire.

Such alliance dynamics may create "intersections" similar to those described in the lateral-pressure model of Choucri and North (1975, see chap. 1, especially for analogues to opportunity and willingness). Choucri and North argue that as the factors of population and technology create greater demands for resources, states expand (in various ways) to acquire the needed resources. The expansion of spheres or areas of control will inevitably come into contact and the probability of conflict increases. Choucri and North (1975, 25) outline the components of their conceptual model as follows:

Expansion: Demands resulting from the interactive effects of population and technological growth give rise to activities beyond national borders.

Conflict of interest: Expanding nations are likely to collide in their activities outside national boundaries; such collisions have some potential for violence.

Military capability: States, by definition, have military establishments; these grow as the result of domestic growth and competition with military establishments of other nations.

Alliance: Nations assess their power, resources, and capabilities in comparison with other nations and attempt to enhance themselves through international alliances.

Violence-behavior: Nations engage in international violence as a consequence of expansion, military capability, and alliances.

Alliances, then, are a key component to the Choucri-North lateral pressure model as well as a separate source of intersections. Although Choucri and North do not treat it as such, their model is essentially a geopolitical one, as it rests on the spatial expansion of the colonial, economic, and resource spheres of states as demonstrated in their analysis of the European powers prior to World War I. In the model proposed (e.g., Choucri and North 1975, 245), the intensity of intersections is positively related to alliances, as is the military expenditures factor. Alliances, in turn, are positively related to violent behavior.

Choucri and North's concept of intersection appears to be similar to O'Sullivan's (1986, 69) concern with the "intersection of force fields." O'Sullivan asserts that conflict will occur in these intersections due to uncertainty. His graphic depiction of such force fields (75) in turn strongly resembles the concepts of unconditional and conditional viability. We can interpret the uncertainty noted by O'Sullivan as deriving from the collision or intersection of spheres or capabilities at some distance from each state, and the lack of clarity over the loss-of-strength gradient effects in any such situation. Alliances allow the projection of capabilities. Alliances are used to facilitate the expansion of spheres of influence or control. Consider, for example, the use the United States has made of the Rio Pact in the Western Hemisphere to control allies and to attempt to legitimize coercion. Such an effect—even in terms of threat—can be fully conceptualized in geopolitical terms.

Another, even more direct, concern with interaction opportunity relates to conflicts that arise over territory. Diehl (1987, 1988) has most recently argued this position (but, see also Weede 1975a, 1975b). Diehl notes (1987, 1): "Scholars too often ignore the most basic of geography's roles in international conflict: as a direct source of conflict. . . . In order to understand the onset and escalation of conflict, it seems that more account must be made of what states are fighting over. In that respect, focusing on territorial concerns as a source of conflict is essential." Diehl then asks *when* will states go to war over some territory, and what characteristics will make some territory worth fighting over?

One answer to Diehl's questions again relates directly to alliances. In 1915 James Fairgrieve developed the concept of the "crush zone," which, as noted by O'Sullivan (1986, 33), described "the belt of small countries lying between the heartland and the sea powers." Following Fairgrieve, O'Sullivan (69) claims that "most of the conflicts of the last thirty years [that is from the mid-1950s to the mid-1980s] have arisen in the crush zone between the great powers." A crush zone could be seen as a buffer zone (e.g., Cohen 1963, 83–84) but also as territory to be fought over, as Diehl suggests. What is not explicitly recognized in the literature, however, is that alliances have either *absorbed* much of what composed the crush zone, as in Central Europe or the informal United States alliance with Israel, or been used to leapfrog crush zones that still acted as buffer zones.[15] One could argue that CENTO was designed to have been used in the latter manner.

Cohen updated Fairgrieve's concept with his own conception of the "shatterbelt," which was a "large, strategically located region that is occupied by a number of conflicting states and is caught between conflicting interests of Great Powers" (Cohen 1963, 83). It, too, constitutes the sort of territory that states fight over. One could think of post–World War II relations between the Western and Eastern blocs and the use of alliances (primarily by the West) as a way both to leapfrog buffer zones and to project Western capability beyond those areas Cohen calls shatterbelts. This, as indicated, was Dulles' strategy of containment.[16]

Thus, alliances may be used to foster proximity and project capabilities. By Walt's argument (1985), this creates a threat. While the threat would be enhanced by ideological factors (to which Walt devotes considerable attention), the geopolitical factors of proximity and the ability to project military capability would appear to be primary bases of the threat.

Alliances: Overcoming Geopolitical Constraints

Conceiving of existing alliances as interaction opportunities is only one form of opportunity derived from environmental possibilism or probabilism. A second form is one we have introduced—how the formation of alliances overcomes geopolitical constraints that face decision makers. That is, if the geopolitical environment, which consists of space, distance, topographical features, and the arrangement of political entities, takes on meaning as a set of constraints on the possibilities and probabilities available to decision makers, alliances may be conceptualized as one mechanism such decision makers may use to cope with or adapt to that environment.

We can use Rosenau's discussion of adaptation (e.g., 1980) as one perspective by which to link entities to their environments. Rosenau comes close to some of the Sproutian notions behind opportunity and willingness when he notes (503): "Considerable insight follows from an initial formulation that conceives national societies—like the single cell, the individual, group, or

---

15. For a useful discussion of buffer states and the role of boundaries in the development and working of the state system, see Kratochwil (1986). It should be noted that O'Sullivan (1986, 70) does recognize the effects of the projection of force by great powers, especially on localized war. However, he does not explicitly link this projection to alliances. The same may be said for Sloan (1988, 214).

16. Cohen (1963), in fact, comes to geopolitical conclusions regarding American cold war strategy for dealing with the Soviets that would have been comfortable for Dulles.

organization—as entities that must adapt to their environments to survive and prosper."[17] If alliances are used to cope with distance, with the military capability of proximate or distant states, or to restructure the incentive structures of allies, enemies or nonaligned states, then alliances are adaptation mechanisms. As Rosenau notes: "Any external behavior undertaken by the government of any national society is adaptive when it copes with, or stimulates, changes in its external environment that contribute to keeping its essential structures within acceptable limits" (1980, 503).

A useful analogy, and one that serves as a transition to the next section, is between alliances and technology. One of the primary reasons that the geographical, or the topographical, constraints that states face are *not* permanent is that they have regularly been overcome or modified by technological innovation in transportation, communication, and military weaponry. Indeed, the revolution in international politics that a number of observers argue has been brought about by nuclear weapons relies just as heavily upon the technological developments in delivery systems as in the weapons themselves. These are systems that have negated the traditional effects of distance and space, of physical barriers such as oceans or mountains. Thus, while water barriers, such as those possessed by the United States or Britain, still provide added security in terms of conventional war, ballistic missile technology makes them meaningless in terms of strategic warfare. In the era of intercontinental ballistic missiles the United States gains little advantage from its ocean barriers, nor does the Soviet Union reap the same benefit from its vast expanses as it did under the czars (or even during World War II).

Harold Sprout argued convincingly (1963, 194) that while Mackinder (1919) and Mahan (1890) both looked at the same geographic reality, their conclusions differed "because of the different weights that each assigned to the properties and significance of advancing technology." Sprout holds that Mahan's view faltered because he failed to pay attention to technological innovation and its effect on the relationship between military capabilities and geography: "Mahan, like so many of his contemporaries, seems to have taken it for granted that the future would not be very different from the immediate past" (Sprout 1963, 194–95).

We have noted that alliances can leapfrog distance and geography. By so doing, alliances also change the meaning of distance, space, and the physical arrangements of the earth's features. But alliances have the advantage of not being dependent on the serendipity of scientific or technological breakthroughs (and the translation of such advances into military, political, or

---

17. In addition, like the ecological triad (or opportunity and willingness), this view of adaptation takes the form of general systems theory, in that adaptation is meant to deal with entity-environment relations across any number of levels of analysis.

economic instruments). Just as we may conceive of alliances as manipulable borders, alliances may also be conceived of as *political technology*. The rapid projection of military capability through diplomacy and treaty formation can render former geopolitical realities meaningless.

Important historic examples would be too numerous to mention, but two attempts may indicate how important such foreign policy activities have been to American policymakers. The German attempt, however feeble, to form some type of political or military coalition with Mexico prior to the American entry into World War I demonstrates the belief that alliance can be used to overcome physical boundaries; and, to preview the next section, the impact of this attempted alliance on American willingness to enter the war indicated how serious a threat this attempt was perceived to be. The Soviet alignment with Cuba subsequent to the Cuban revolution has had very similar aims and reactions, especially during the 1960s. The attempt to use a form of alliance to permit the projection of military capability and overcome geography, and the threat it created, is well reflected in all the accounts of the 1962 Cuban missile crisis. It is almost as if decision makers implicitly recognize the limitations inherent in the loss-of-strength gradient and seek to mitigate these through the use of alliances permitting the projection of power in ways that otherwise would not be possible.

In sum, alliances are similar to technology as a mechanism to overcome geopolitical constraints, and as a way to alter the menu of incentives, costs, and benefits that exists in the international system. The key difference, of course, is that alliances are the result of conscious choice through diplomatic activity. Alliances are more manipulable than borders; alliances are more predictable and reliable than technological change. Decision makers are thus willing to create alliances, to honor alliances (or give them up), and to accept the geopolitical consequences of their creation.

Alliances and Willingness

Two general relationships between alliances and willingness within a geopolitical context are introduced here. The first derives from the broad question of why states are willing to enter alliances in the first place. Joining an alliance entails the potential of great risks as well as benefits. Any decision that indicates the willingness to enter an alliance indicates that the joining state expects greater benefits than costs (at least in the short run; see Huth and Russett 1988), that the expected utility derived from joining the alliance is greater than eschewing the alliance possibility. Why do states enter alliances? Walt (1985) focuses primarily on alliance formation as a response to threat— that states balance or hop on a bandwagon with others as a mechanism for dealing with their perceptions of external threat. Starr (1978b) surveys a variety of reasons why states ally. While a number of reasons are directly related to capabilities and security issues (and thus directly or indirectly to threat), other reasons cannot be so clearly connected. One reason states ally is for the aggregation of military capability. States also seek allies in order to preempt such states from joining the alliances of others. States may ally in order to take advantage of the strategic position of the ally. While the first two reasons are concerned with the addition (or subtraction) of overall military capabilities, the last reason is directly related to adapting to the geopolitical environment.

Alliances may also be formed to meet a deterrent or balancing function. Alliances may add precision to state relations and thus make a deterrent threat clearer (and more credible); the aggregation of the military capabilities of several states may also make deterrent threats more credible. Credibility may be enhanced by the projection of military capability if that capability can serve as trip wires that will trigger extended deterrence. Thus, the projection of power permitted by alliances may serve aggressive or defensive functions and have threatening and provocative consequences or deterrent consequences.[18]

Alliances also entail risks—that the deterrent threat will be challenged, that the alliance will drag a partner into conflicts it would prefer to ignore, that rash or obstreperous alliance partners will create situations that will involve other alliance members. In essence, alliances serve as conduits along which conflict may flow. Alliances create commitments that states may be called upon to honor, with a failure to do so involving a loss of credibility.

If we are concerned with why states are willing to join alliances, we thus have a wide range of possible answers. For many states, however, the risks of alliance are taken because they are offset by the military or security benefits alliances seem to provide. The risks are accepted because of the opportunities that alliances provide—opportunities that occur because of the ability of alliances to override the geopolitical constraints of the international system. Balancing, bandwagoning, aggregating capabilities, and projecting capabilities all provide such opportunities.

Recent work by Huth and Russett (1984, 1988), building on earlier research by Russett (1963), develops an expected utility model with which to study extended deterrence. One relationship they investigate is the willingness of a defender to come to the aid of a protege. If deterrence fails, if the attacker ignores a deterrent threat, does the defender actually come to the defense of

---

18. States may also join alliances to control allies (including the maintenance of the governments of allies), to legitimate in their domestic political arenas unilateral activities such as intervention, for a variety of collective (stability, order, deterrence) or private (economic or military aid, help against a specific opponent, to maintain domestic control) goods. For examples of more formal analyses of coalition or alliance formation, see such works as Gamson (1961), Riker (1962), or Snyder and Diesing (1977).

the protege? In this event the existence of a formal alliance has a strong relationship to actual defense. Huth and Russett (1984, 521) report that "without an alliance the chances the defender would fight were only about two in three; with an alliance, virtually unity."

This work relates directly to the conceptualization of alliances as policy preferences or positions of policy preference. In this sense, states indicate they are willing to ally with others—willing to incur the risks of alliance (including those involved with extended deterrence)—because of similarity of policy preference. The Huth and Russett finding suggests that alliances indicate a willingness to make commitments and to fulfill them. States, then, are willing to commit to explicit security interdependence because of the existence of other military, political, economic, or cultural interdependence.

Alliances are and have been an important component of international politics. While some think that their character may be altering amid the rapid changes taking place in the contemporary international system (Kegley and Raymond 1990), it is useful to remember that the importance we have attached to alliances is chiefly as a device for estimating an underlying variable, willingness. To be sure, we believe that alliances in themselves can, as we argued, have a pronounced effect on the geopolitical context within which states make calculations about their foreign policy choices, but notwithstanding this, they were primarily used as a measure of the willingness of one nation to join its foreign policy to that of some other nation or nations. In a sense, they tell us about the proximity of one state's foreign policy to that of some other nation or nations. More importantly, they tell us about the state's willingness to be publicly identified as allied with some other nation or nations.

Using alliances to measure this over a lengthy period has several advantages, not the least of which is the ready availability of the data. In addition, since the alliances in the data set have all been ratified by member states, it is clear that they represent matters of serious policy deliberation and choice. Even if legislative ratification is not present or if it takes place in an authoritarian context, ratification carries with it a formal document with mutual obligations. It may be disavowed, but its existence cannot be denied to the other party or parties. Finally, alliances carried with them the costs of sharing foreign policy with other nations. Put differently, amity and shared policy with one nation usually leads to or follows from enmity with others. It thereby reduces a state's room to maneuver.

The problems of using alliances are clear. Alliances frequently outlive the span of the shared policies. Policies may be shared on some issues, but not others. They may indicate greater policy sharing than actually exists. Some alliances may have more to do with gaining the acquiescence of the partner to goals that are unrelated to shared interests (Levy 1981). Some alliances may be fairly characterized as cynically insincere. We must admit that the enumeration of the difficulties of alliances as a measure of willingness could go on further, but in the end one is hard-pressed to find another available indicator that would cover a long time span, involve serious state policy, and not be subject to difficulties of its own that are just as great or even greater.

Decision makers have been willing to use alliances to overcome the constraints of geopolitics; they have been willing to accept the risks that alliances, as interaction opportunities, bring. They have been willing because those opportunities also hold many potential benefits. They have been willing because as alliances indicate important policy congruencies between the partners, they indicate that partners may have greater salience to each other that is worth the risks of conflict with third parties.

Conclusion

In this chapter we have elaborated the geopolitical context within which one can conceptualize alliances. Following the advice of Most and Starr (1989), we have consciously tried to ask what alliances are *about* in the investigation of geopolitics and diffusion in order to place our empirical work into a broader conceptual and theoretical context. This context is most broadly characterized by the opportunity and willingness framework. This chapter has also attempted to indicate a sample of work by political scientists and geographers that may be related to alliance as a concept useful for the geopolitical study of diffusion and international conflict, providing a fuller and more explicit context for continued work in this area.

While we will be concerned in this book with the growth of war and alliances as a factor in that growth, the geopolitical context outlined here may also help us generate additional research questions. For example, we may seek to discover whether geographical proximity makes any difference in alliance behavior. That is, does greater opportunity increase willingness? One way of looking at this question is to examine the alliance choices of nations. If opportunity enhances willingness, then we would expect to find that states that share some type of border have a greater probability of alliance than those that do not. However, it must be recognized that states often enter into alliances because they seek to enhance their security and that not all potential partners are able to offer the same security benefits as all others. The states that have the greatest range of choice are the major powers, since, by definition, they have the most power and power is what is usually deemed to buy security, particularly for others.

The question now becomes: To what extent were the alliance choices of the major powers directed toward states on their borders? While we as yet cannot present a complete answer to this question, it is noteworthy that, with the exception of the northern countries in the German confederation, Austria-Hungary never entered into an alliance with a minor power with which it was not contiguous and that it was not until the 1930s that the United Kingdom entered into an alliance with a minor power with which it was not contiguous across open water and fairly close. In other words, contiguity seems to have had a powerful effect on alliance choices when there was a difference in power.

Alliances may be studied at a number of different levels of analysis and to deal with a number of different questions about international politics. By placing the study of alliances within a geopolitical context, we have attempted to specify the meaning of alliances in terms of opportunity and willingness, and to indicate how this context provides a coherent focus for current and future research.

CHAPTER 3

The Diffusion of War across Space, 1816–1965

Chapter 2 presented our basic ideas concerning the application of opportunity and willingness to the spread of international conflict. In this chapter we use historical data to assess the impact of these factors on the diffusion of international war between 1816 and 1965. Specifically, we seek to explore the extent to which different amounts of opportunity, as measured by various numbers and kinds of borders, and different levels of willingness, as measured by varying numbers and kinds of alliances, will affect national propensities to join ongoing wars. The design of our data collection procedures will allow us to make such estimates based upon the extent to which a state either is or is not exposed to warring border nations (WBNs) or warring alliances partners (WAPs), which we consider as *treatments*.[1]

After presenting the research problem and outlining our data collection procedures and sources, we will offer a brief description of the diffusion of war before moving to the major task of this chapter, measuring the effect of opportunity and willingness on the diffusion of war.

The Problem

In order to differentiate positive spatial diffusion from both reinforcement phenomena and negative spatial diffusion, we derived and tested a set of expectations about the effects of borders and alliances on the war-joining rates

---

1. The use of the term *treatment* may appear as either odd or inappropriate. To be sure, this term is more frequently found in experimental science where an investigator is able to control the amount of the experimental variable that randomly determined cases will receive. Under such an arrangement, the posttreatment differences among the cases are attributed to the effects of the variable. While some investigators may speak of history as the "laboratory of conflict" (Holsti and North 1965), we are all too aware that there are limits within this laboratory and that at least one of these is lack of randomization in the assignment of variables to cases. Nonetheless, over the last two decades social science has witnessed the emergence of quasi-experimental research, which allows investigators to explore research designs that are somewhere between the experimental and observational. This is often accomplished through the construction of data collection methods that permit the control of variables that previously could be studied only through statistical controls.

of states. The procedure used here is descended from one used in an earlier study by Starr and Most (1983, 110–11).[2] In their design they begin by

> looking for all states at any given point in time which were at peace (to avoid complications with "reinforcement" effects) and asked two questions: (1) At that point in time did they have any warring border nations? (2) Within the next five years did they have any new war participation?

There is one major deviation in the present study from the design set out here. Instead of looking at a treatment at time t_0 and subsequent behavior only during the t_1–t_5 period, we have looked at all years (t_0) in which the international system was experiencing interstate war (some eighty-three years between 1816 and 1965) and examined the extent to which nations not at war in $t - 1$ either were or were not exposed to various combinations of WBNs or WAPs and either did or did not go to war in year t_0. Recall that once a nation enters a war, it is removed from the data set until the war is ended or the nation leaves the war. Under this procedure it is possible then to aggregate the results of all war years for each of the treatments.

This procedure made it possible for us to estimate and compare the effects of various combinations of WBNs and WAPs. Moreover, by running identical tables for the conditions of *any border* or *any alliance*, we were able to estimate the extent to which WBNs and WAPs made a difference over counterpart conditions where war as a condition or treatment was absent. That is, we could compare the effects of having a contiguous WBN to the effects of simply having contiguous border nations; or compare the effects of having a defense pact WAP to the effects of simply having defense pact partners. Delineating the effects of the various types and combinations of borders and alliances *without* WBNs or WAPs thus gives us a set of baselines for comparing the war-joining rate of those states *with* bordering states at war (WBNs) and/or alliance partners that were at war (WAPs).

The logic of our investigation of diffusion centers on the notion of *treatment*—that the environment of the decision makers of states will have been changed by the existence of war in a bordering nation or in one of its alliance partners. As discussed in chapter 2, such treatments may alter both the opportunities facing decision makers and their willingness to pursue cer-

---

2. Recall that Most and Starr (1980) distinguished between reinforcement, sometimes called addiction (where a state's war behavior affects the probability of its *own* subsequent behavior) and diffusion (where a state's war behavior affects the probability of the subsequent war behavior of other states). They also recognized that either could have positive (increasing the probability of war behavior) or negative (decreasing that probability) effects. The reader must be alerted that the matrix employed in our analyses follows that utilized in Most et al. (1990) and *is not the same* as the matrix used in Most and Starr (1981) or Starr and Most (1983, 110–11).

Treatment

		Absent	Present
War Participation	Absent	a	b
	Present	c	d

Fig. 3.1. The border-alliance treatment matrix

tain behavioral alternatives, such as going to war. The argument also follows our notions that states' interactions will tend to follow along the paths provided by interaction opportunities such as proximity (borders) and common policy interests or high value salience (alliances).

Our expectations on the effects of such treatments also may be seen within a *loose necessity* framework. That is, these treatments are to be seen as loosely necessary but not sufficient for influencing the war-joining behavior of states. We are arguing not that such treatments always lead to joining ongoing wars but that war behavior is much more likely to occur if such treatments have occurred; thus, the *loose* aspect of the logically necessary relationship between treatment and consequence. The key to these expectations is cell *d* in figure 3.1, which sets out our basic treatment matrix. Cell *d* indicates that a state has joined a war subsequent to being exposed to the relevant treatment. The central expectation is that there should be a clear and strong difference in cell *d* between matrices where there is a treatment and matrices where there is *no* treatment. That is, analyses presented will contrast the results found in a matrix where the columns simply note the presence or absence of *borders* or *alliances* to the results of a matrix that looks like the one presented in figure 3.1, where *warring* border nations or *warring* alliance partners comprise the treatment columns.

This is a simple idea: being exposed to a treatment will, using Alcock's (1972) phrase, increase the chances of "catching the war disease." We ask what the world should *look like* if a state has a bordering state at war or an alliance partner at war. Our expectation is that a WBN or WAP should substantially increase the probability of that state joining the ongoing war of its WBN or WAP. A further expectation is that this probability should increase with the combination of border and alliance treatments. Thus, we have taken one of several possible approaches to diffusion—the growth of ongoing wars. We have identified two possible (loosely necessary) agents by which those wars would grow. We have then posited a simple expectation of behavior given treatments by those agents. The findings presented below present data that simply, but directly, test these expectations.

The Data

In order to evaluate the impact of WBNs and WAPs on the diffusion of war, we constructed a data set containing several types of information on national borders, national alliance commitments, and national war participation. Data were collected and coded in order to test both a warring border nation hypothesis and a warring alliance partner hypothesis. Thus, the WBN hypothesis and the WAP hypothesis may be tested separately, and the strength of the results compared. The data also permit us to look at the impact of a nation's bordering states that were *also* allies. This will enable us to test the combined, interactive effect of a state's having both a warring border nation and a warring alliance partner. Again, the results of these analyses may be compared to the results of the analyses of each factor singly. We compare the magnitude of the effect of each variable or combination of variables by looking at the differences produced when the variable or variables are present versus baseline cases in which they are absent.

To make the appropriate comparisons, however, it is necessary to do more than simply record the relevant border and alliance information for those instances in which nations entered a war. Doing so would tell us something about the process of diffusion, but such a procedure would deal only with successful cases in which diffusion took place. Those cases in which a nation experienced some type of either a WBN or a WAP but did not enter the war would be lost from view and hence no estimate could be made of the possible effect of the variable on the larger population within which these nations exist (see Most and Starr 1989, especially chaps. 3–5).

Information on the set of states in the system, war participation, and national alliance commitments was relatively easy to acquire. The set of states was taken from the lists provided in Small and Singer (1982) as part of their analysis of the correlates of war. We also noted the power status of the various nations, using a simple division of states into either major power or minor power status.[3]

There are, of course, several generally available data sets on international war, including, most notably, those of Richardson (1960), Wright (1965), Kende (1971, 1978) and Small and Singer (1982). The initial Most and Starr (1980) diffusion analyses used a combination of all these sources, as their analyses, in actuality, investigated the diffusion of any organized violent conflict (whether it was civil war, internal conflict, or intervention; or rela-

---

3. Following Small and Singer (1982), the major powers and the years of their inclusion in that group are Austria-Hungary (1816–1918), Italy (1861–1943), the United Kingdom (1816–1965), Russia/USSR (1816–1965), Japan (1895–1945), Prussia/Germany (1816/1945), United States (1898–1965), France (1816–1940 and 1945–65) and China (1949–65).

tively small-scale violence) as well as large-scale organized interstate violence.

The present research, however, focuses on interstate war not just for some relatively brief period but for the entire state system over the post-Napoleonic era to 1965.[4] We thus selected the larger-scale interstate war data set presented in Small and Singer (1982), which represents an updating and refinement of a well-established, highly regarded earlier effort by the same authors (Singer and Small 1972) as part of their project on the Correlates of War. We consider the Correlates of War data as representing large-scale organized conflict because of the criteria employed delineating occurrence, national participation, and outcome. As explained by Small and Singer (1982, chap. 2) interstate or intrasystemic wars require at least one member of the international system on each of the two sides, with various combinations of population and/or diplomatic recognition criteria needing to be met in order to be recognized as a member of the international system. Not only must participants meet a set of political status requirements, but they also need to meet one of two participation requirements: "either a minimum of 100 battle fatalities, or a minimum of 1,000 armed personnel engaged in active combat within the war theater" (Small and Singer 1982, 55). For any specific hostility to qualify as an interstate war, a minimum of 1,000 battle fatalities for all participating system members is required.

There were several reasons to select this war data set. First, it incorporates a great deal of the information contained in the earlier studies by Wright (1965) and Richardson (1960). The data used here cover more contemporary events than the compilations by Wright and Richardson but also cover much earlier periods than the post–1945 data of others (e.g., Kende). Finally, utilizing the Small and Singer data will make our findings compatible with the growing body of empirical work that has derived from the Correlates of War Project (e.g., Gochman and Sabrosky 1990a).

---

4. Ideally, we would have brought the data set up to 1990 or some other point more recent than 1965. While this was our desire, we were sharply constrained by the fact that alliance data after 1965 are not readily available. Getting them on our own, instead of using an already available source such as we have done with the Correlates of War data, would have required resources beyond those we had available, almost all of which went toward generating the border data between 1816 and 1946. (Remember that Most and Starr had already gathered border data between 1946 and 1965). Some may think that gathering alliance data is an easy thing to do; with no disrespect to them, those who believe this have not likely tried to do it. These pragmatic issues obscure a more important point. Our intention is to explore the utility of a theoretical approach to international conflict. Our intent is not to *describe* the contemporary international system. Adding a few years to our data set may provide the appearance of timeliness and relevance, but it would not necessarily add to the analysis. Put differently, after looking at 150 years of data, what do we expect to have happened between 1965 and, say, 1980 to upset, nullify, or radically change the findings?

The alliance data also are a product of the Correlates of War Project. In this case we drew upon Sabrosky's (1975) extensive revision of an earlier work by Singer and Small (1968) that provided an initial listing of formal international alliances among states during the period, 1815–1965. In the case of each alliance, we identified its class as coded by Singer and Small; that is, defense agreements, neutrality pacts, or ententes. These will be referred to as A1, A2, or A3, respectively.

We view these types of alliance commitments as forming a rough ordinal index of willingness. Sabrosky's (1980, 171–72) discussion outlines these three types of alliances as developed by the Correlates of War Project:

> The strongest alliance commitment is a defense pact . . . in which the signatories agree to intervene militarily in the event of an attack on one of their number. Next, insofar as the formal strength of the alliance is concerned, is the neutrality or nonaggression pact . . . which obligates the signatories to remain militarily neutral should one of them become involved in a war. . . . Finally, the entente . . . merely required [*sic*] consultations or conversations if one of the signatories was attacked.

Thus we expect that WAPs involving defensive alliances, A1, will have a greater likelihood of producing diffusion, than nonaggression pacts, A2, or finally the ententes, A3. However, we recognize and will see in chapter 4 that there are limitations to the strength of this ordering. Moreover, some of the groupings may be too broad. For example, Levy (1981, 588) contends:

> Whereas the neutrality pact generally obligates each signatory to remain militarily neutral in the event of an attack on the other, and may even designate specific aggressors to which the alliance is applicable, the more sweeping non-aggression pact is simply an assurance that neither will use force against the other.

To be sure, this observation is correct. However, it really is an objection to the coarseness of the measurement employed. Any measure may be more refined. The question is, what is gained by the cost of doing so?

The most difficult data to gather were those indicating which states shared borders and for how long. However, through the use of several excellent historical atlases (Shepherd 1932; *Hammond Historical Atlas* 1984), it was possible to ascertain the border network of states back to 1815. Specifically, in a modified version of the coding rules used by Starr and Most (1976), we recorded for each state those national entities (1) on its contiguous borders, (2) across less than 200 miles of open water, and (3) on the borders of its colonial possessions. We refer to these as B1, B2, or B3, respectively. A full description and justification of these border operationalizations has been presented elsewhere (Starr and Most 1976). Briefly, both the cross-water and colonial possession borders were included because of their combined impact on salience of and ease of interaction with neighbors, as discussed earlier.

Just as in the case of the alliance variables, we regard the divisions of the border variables as having an ordinal value. In terms of the opportunity and willingness concepts we have discussed we hypothesize that the greatest opportunity is present with contiguous borders, then with cross-water borders, and finally with colonial borders (Starr and Most 1976).

The data on war participation and alliance membership are available in the sources we have cited. The data we gathered on borders are presented in the appendix to this book.

Setting the Problem

Our initial data set consists of records for all national entities contained in the Small and Singer list of nations-states for the period 1816–1965. This full data set consisted of 6,250 nation years of data. However, recall that our interest is in explaining not the initial outbreak of war between nations but how it may spread once it begins, so that in our analysis we have no interest in data from any year in which a war either did not start or was not ongoing. Accordingly we deleted the data for all nonwar years. We also deleted the data for the first two nations to begin fighting in any war and the data for all the joining nations for the years after that in which they joined the war. Thus, for example, Germany and Poland are not included for 1939. Britain and France are included for 1939 but are removed for 1940–45.[5] Nations that joined a war on one side and then changed sides continued to be deleted after their initial joining. For example, Italy is deleted from the data set between 1941 and 1945, although in 1944 it left the war and then rejoined. All these procedures work against our hypotheses; that is, the deletion of these cases

---

5. Also removed in 1939 are Finland, which fought the Soviet Union, and the Soviet Union, which fought Finland and Japan. Japan is removed from 1937 to 1945 because it began fighting China in the former year. Copies of the coding scheme employed in this study are available from Siverson at the Department of Political Science, University of California, Davis. It should be noted that in general we followed the data given by Small and Singer (1982) with respect to war expansion. We did, however, depart from their delineation of what constituted war joining in a few cases. For example, they show Japan as joining World War II on December 7, 1941. While it is true that Japan began fighting the United States on that day, it is also true that the Japanese decision had relatively less to do with the European war that had been in progress since 1939 than it did to Japan's war with China that had been ongoing since 1937. Hence, we do not treat Japan as joining the war. Also we do not treat as war joiners those nations that left World War II (albeit briefly) and then changed sides (namely, Italy, Rumania, and Bulgaria) to reenter the war. It makes sense to count the initial participation only. It should be noted that including these cases would have favored the opportunity and willingness hypotheses.

works against our hypotheses, because the nations were involved in war and thus more likely to turn up in the treatment category.

The final data set consists of 3,749 nation years; that is, there were 3,749 nations eligible to join a war once the first two nations began fighting. There were, however, only 94 cases of war diffusion. The overall rate of diffusion is thus 2.51 percent, a rate that is rather small. Perhaps it might even be called rare; but whether it is rare or small does not mean it is unimportant. Many statistically rare events are of considerable interest to scientists, particularly when their consequences are either highly lethal or very costly. For example, both lung cancer and earthquakes are relatively rare but are nonetheless the objects of attention for very large, nationally organized research efforts. As noted in chapter 1, war diffusion is both lethal and costly. Of the 221 cases of international war involvement of any kind in the Singer-Small data set between 1816 and 1965, the 94 cases we study here represent 42.8 percent of the total. Additionally, as noted earlier, a great deal of the severity of war (i.e., how many die) may be explained in terms of the expansion or growth of war. From the data in Small and Singer's (1982) consideration of lethality in warfare, it is clear that most of the war-related deaths take place because of war expansion. Again, as noted, it is often the largest wars that have the most profound consequences for the organization of the international system (Siverson 1980).

Because war diffusion is a relatively rare event, it may be seen that under loose necessity a large number of treatments result in a much smaller number of cases of war diffusion. In this respect several points should be noted. First, in this chapter we investigate only one form of diffusion, infection, or the growth of an ongoing war; we do not deal with demonstration effects. Also if *only* the opportunity for interaction were of concern, we might expect ongoing wars to grow to include all those states with opportunity. However, willingness is important in such decisions. Put differently, decision makers choose behavior within the constraints posed by the range of incentive structures within which they are imbedded; the effects of warring border nations and warring alliance partners are just one aspect of that structure. While other aspects of the structure may lead to the willingness to choose other foreign policy behaviors, it is impressive that the opportunity and willingness model of interaction opportunity is able to identify WBNs and WAPs as factors having a significant impact on war-joining behavior.

Data Analysis

This part of the data analysis will take place in three stages. First, we will examine the extent to which war diffusion may be accounted for by a simple model involving only the effects of time. Second, we will explore the extent to which the variables measuring opportunity and willingness have a discernable effect on war expansion. Put differently, we will show that there is a significant relationship between the measures of opportunity and willingness and national proclivities to join a war. Both borders and alliances play a role in the geopolitical context of states and serve as agents of interaction opportunity, as pointed out in chapter 2. As such, we could hypothesize that they would have stronger combined interactive effects than either alone. Thus, the third part of our data analysis will examine the manner in and degree to which various individual and combined treatments affect war-joining behavior. The next chapter will attempt to account for the length of time that it takes for a nation to join a war.

The Diffusion of War and the Passage of Time

One thing that can be noted in an examination of data describing international war is that large wars, that is, wars with many participants, seem to last a good deal longer than wars with relatively few participants. There is a straightforward explanation for such a pattern: The longer a war goes on, the greater the chances that something will happen to draw in other participants. In view of this possibility one question we need to ask is how much war diffusion can be accounted for purely in terms of the length of a war.

One way of answering this question is simply to find the correlation between war length, as measured in months, and war size. Figure 3.2 displays a plot of the data for this relationship for the 54 wars in the entire Small and Singer data set on international war. The Pearson correlation for these data is .41. However, there are two things to note about the distribution of the data. First, there is an outlier in the upper right of the plot that exerts an undue influence on the size of the correlation.[6] If the data are transformed by adding one to each variable and taking its log, the influence of the outlier is reduced (but not eliminated) and the correlation falls to .22. Second, there is a relatively large number of cases in which wars went on for some time without growing beyond two initial participants or grew only slightly. One conclusion emerges from these observations. The passage of time accounts for remarkably little of the size of a war; in fact, for the transformed data, time explains slightly less than 5 percent of the size of a war.

Do Opportunity and Willingness Influence
War Diffusion?

If time does not account for the growth of a war, to what extent do opportunity and willingness account for it? From the previous discussion of opportunity and willingness it is obvious that we expect that nations that have been

---

6. The outlier is marked by a 2 in the plot; the 2 represents its influence on the relationship.

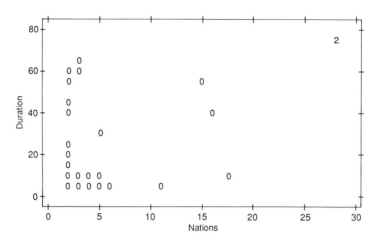

Fig. 3.2. Plot of war length and number of nations in the war

exposed to either WBNs or WAPs will have a higher propensity to join a war than those that have not. We begin our analysis by examining the extent to which this expectation is borne out. Table 3.1 reports two initial parts of this analysis. The top of the table presents the cross-tabulation of a nation's having *any* border or *any* alliance and being a war joiner. Except for the fifteen cases in the left column, this baseline is the same as the overall baseline. It is readily apparent that the table contains no relationship.[7] Moving to the bottom section of the table, it may be seen that when a nation is exposed to any of the treatments, the propensity to join a war increases substantially over those that are not exposed. Put simply, in the baseline case 2.4 percent of the nations participate, but under the treatments 6.1 percent join.

While the lower section demonstrates that exposure to any treatment increases the likelihood of joining a war, we need to examine the effect of increasing numbers of treatments. Nations may at the same time have various types of warring borders, be the members of several alliances of different types having members in the war, or, more likely, have some combination of warring borders and alliances. Table 3.2 displays the cross-tabulation of war involvement against the number of treatments to which a state was exposed. It is clear from the data that as the amount of exposure increases, the rate of

7. The single case of war involvement by a nation with no bordering nations of any kind and no alliance involvement is New Zealand's entry into World War II in 1939. It might, however, be argued that even this case fits into the willingness logic with which we have characterized alliances. It could be contended that the British Commonwealth—with its bonds of common history, culture, and traditions among the former dominions and explicit common allegiance to the British sovereign—served at least the same functions (or more) as an entente.

TABLE 3.1.   No Treatment, Treatments, and War Involvement, 1816–1965

War Involvement	No Treatment Border or Alliance	
	No	Yes
No	14	3,641
Yes	1	93

War Involvement	Treatments Warring Border Nation or Warring Alliance Partner	
	No	Yes
No	2,320	1,335
Yes	8	86

participation increases as well. The overall relationship, as measured by the correlation ratio (eta), derived from a one-way analysis of variance, is .452. Note that over 62 percent of those cases with five or more treatments became involved in war. Contrast this to only 1.2 percent for those exposed to just one treatment (the only number of treatments that does less well than the no-war treatments reported in table 3.1).

What the analysis has not thus far clarified is which of the variables makes the greatest difference. There are, unfortunately, some difficulties in making such an assessment. Our dependent variable, war involvement, is dichotomous, which means that the usual techniques of regression and cor-

TABLE 3.2.   War Diffusion and Number of Treatments to which a Nation Was Exposed

War Involvement	Number of Treatments							
	0	1	2	3	4	5	6	> 6
No	2,320	703	372	142	57	34	12	15
Yes	8	9	17	12	10	16	7	15
Percentage Yes	0.3	1.2	4.3	7.8	14.9	32.0	36.8	50.0

Variance $R^2 = 18.737$, $\bar{R} = 1.441$, $df = 13$[a]
               (72.906)   (0.20)   (3735)

$F = 73.839$
$p = < .001$
$\eta = .452$

[a]The degrees-of-freedom are from the uncollapsed table.

TABLE 3.3 Probit Estimates of Treatment Variables on
War Involvement, 1816–1965

Parameter	Estimate	t-statistic	p
Constant	−2.6162	−31.795	
B1	0.5431	9.971	< .01
B2	0.3629	3.472	< .02
B3	0.2115	3.766	< .01
A1	0.5123	5.684	< .01
A2	0.1758	1.362	> .10
A3	0.3070	3.139	< .05

relation are not appropriate. Normally one could approach this type of a problem with log-linear analysis, but an analysis based upon dichotomies of the six possible independent variables and war involvement would produce a table of 128 cells. Given the large total number of observations we have, this would not ordinarily be a problem, but in this instance only 94 of the cases indicate war diffusion, and allocating these in a very large table will produce such a large number of empty cells that analysis is questionable.

Fortunately, it is possible to gain estimates of the effects of the various independent variables on war diffusion through probit, which although sensitive to the highly skewed distribution of the data will allow us to make a preliminary comparison of the relative effect of the variables on war diffusion. Table 3.3 displays the results of the probit analysis when a state's war involvement is analyzed in relation to its (1) number of contiguous warring bordering nations, B1, (2) number of cross-water warring bordering nations, B2, (3) number of colonial warring bordering nations, B3, (4) number of warring defense alliance partners, A1, (5) number of warring neutrality agreement partners, A2, and (6) number of warring entente partners, A3. The estimates it gives for the independent variables are generally equivalent to the estimates of Beta reported in regressions. The results given in table 3.3 are generally consistent with the ideas of opportunity and willingness. That is, for the border variables B1 has greater weight in influencing war joining than B2, and B2 has more than B3. The alliance variables are slightly different. While A1 counts the most of these variables, A3 influences war joining much more than A2; in fact, from this analysis A2 seems to have little or no effect on war joining.[8]

---

8. The weak results from A2 may be partly due to the fact that there were far fewer of this type of alliance in the data set than either of the other two types. When they are analyzed together, the more numerous alliances may overwhelm A2. In the analysis that follows it may be seen that A2 does not apply to a large number of cases, but that when it does a clear effect is evident. There is also some debate as to exactly how the rigidity and flexibility of these two forms of alliance

How Much Do the Variables Contribute
to War Diffusion?

Thus far our analysis has indicated that any exposure to the treatment variables substantially increases the chances of a nation joining a war (table 3.1), that more exposure increases such chances (table 3.2), and that the strength of the impact of the treatment variables is ordered approximately as our rationale for opportunity and willingness suggested (table 3.3). What the analysis has not revealed is the magnitude of the impact of the individual and combined indicators of opportunity and willingness. It is to that subject that we now turn.

Let us begin with a brief, but necessary, description of the relatively straightforward analysis that follows. Recall from table 3.1 that we compared the rate of war joining among all nations to that of only those nations that had been exposed to at least one treatment variable. We may now, in effect, take the top and bottom sections of tables 3.1 apart and examine the impact of each of the variables individually on war diffusion and then combine each of the border variables with each of the alliance variables to observe their combined impact on war diffusion.

Table 3.4 reports the results for all nations of being exposed to one of the three types of WBNs or WAPs, the *baseline result* and the *percentage change* associated with the treatment.[9] Beginning with borders, two things are appar-

---

might affect the behavior of member states. This issue is addressed with the analyses presented in chapter 4.

9. Recall the treatment matrix from figure 3.1. In the single treatment tables that follow, the numbers being reported are those from cell *d* of that figure. Reporting all the figures would be cumbersome, so only the effects of the treatments are given. As an example of what a matrix looks like, we offer the following full matrix for the *treatment* involving B1:

Contiguous WBN

		Absent	Present
War Participation	Absent	2,950	705
		a	b
	Present	27	67
		c	d
	Totals	2,977	722

Note that the *N*s reported in the tables refer to the total of the *b-d* column and that the percentages reported are for *d* of that total.

TABLE 3.4.   Effects of Individual Border and Alliance Treatments for All Nations, 1816–1965

| Condition | Cell *d* Percentage | | Percent Change |
	No Treatment	Treatment	
B1	2.4	8.7	+262**
	(N = 3,300)	(N = 772)	
B2	3.1	9.2	+196**
	(N = 1,696)	(N = 295)	
B3	2.6	5.6	+115**
	(N = 1,992)	(N = 659)	
A1	5.3	28.6	+439**
	(N = 808)	(N = 105)	
A2	4.4	17.5	+297
	(N = 204)	(N = 40)	
A3	4.2	11.2	+166**
	(N = 453)	(N = 160)	

Test of significance:
Difference of proportions, ** = $p < .01$

ent. First, the presence of a WBN has a significant impact on war diffusion. In each case the presence of the treatment produces a marked increase in the propensity for diffusion, ranging from a 262 percent increase for the contiguous borders to slightly over 100 percent for the colonial borders.[10] Second, the strength of the results is ordered in the manner in which the opportunity hypothesis predicts, with the closest borders producing the strongest result and the most distant producing the weakest.[11]

Turning to the alliance variables shown in table 3.4, a similar pattern may be seen, but with considerably stronger results. Defense alliances produce the substantial increase of 439 percent over the baseline. While the results for neutrality agreements and ententes are weaker—297 and 166 percent, respectively—they are still strong. Again the strength of the relationships is ordered from the strongest to the weakest commitments. As agents of

10. What we mean by percentage increase is the magnitude by which involvement in a treatment situation is larger than the base. Thus, in table 3.4, while the B1 treatment percentage of 8.7 is more than three times the size of the baseline percentage of 2.4, the relevant measurement is the amount of increase from 2.4 to 8.7. Thus the appropriate calculation is the treatment percent minus the base percent with the remainder divided by the base percent.

11. The tests of significance used in tables 3.4 and 3.5 require a brief comment. Because the percentage changes between the no treatment and treatment columns are often based on relatively small numbers of cases, the skeptical reader may be curious as to (1) whether the observed changes are statistically significant, and (2) whether there is any way that the method could fail to produce a change (i.e., are the results predetermined?). With respect to the first question, we have tested the differences for statistical significance in two ways. First, when the *N*

the opportunity for interaction, both borders and alliances meet the expectation of increasing the probability of states joining ongoing wars. In addition to the increased ease of interaction that borders provide (opportunity), borders and alliances both individually increase the salience of the WAPs and WBNs, and thus also the willingness to become involved in their conflicts.

How do the border and alliance variables interact with each other? The three border and three alliance variables combine, of course, to produce nine possibilities. Table 3.5 reports the results of these combinations for all nations. (Because the tables reporting the combination of the variables contain eight cells, the cell corresponding to *d* in figure 3.1 is *h*.) It may readily be seen that there is a considerable amount of interaction between the border and alliance variables in influencing the diffusion of war. The most potent effect is with the combination of the contiguous WBNs and defensive WAPs. This should not be surprising given our previous results and our hierarchy of importance within opportunity and willingness. The latter derives clearly from the international relations literature. Most geopolitical studies focus upon direct, contiguous borders because of their immediate impact and because they provide the most important opportunity for interaction. In turn, the form of alliance that scholars theorize creates the strongest bond between states is the defensive pact. Defense pacts provide the most important indicator of salience, commitment, and shared policy preference. The magnitude of the joint effect is, to say the least, considerable, with the combination of these two variables producing an increase of 719 percent over the baseline cases in producing war diffusion.

While that result is the strongest, the other results on the several combined variables also generally reveal a considerable amount of interaction. Indeed, *all* contiguous border (B1) and all noncolony cross-water (B2) effects are improved when combined with alliance variables; all defense and neutrality pact (A1 and A2) effects are improved when combined with B1 and B2. Cross-water WBNs and defense WAPs, for example, combine to produce an increase of 602 percent over the baseline cases, while cross-water WBNs and neutrality WAPs combine to increase war diffusion 566 percent over the

---

in the treatment column is greater than 20, the *p* value is derived from the Z score in a test of a difference of proportions. When the *N* is less than 20, we have determined the *p* value from Fisher's exact test. (Recall that the cases in the treatment column are also present in the baseline no treatment column. Because the two results are therefore not independent, before we could test for statistical significance between the no treatment baseline and the treatment, it was necessary to remove the treatment cases from their respective baseline.) More important than each test of significance is the correspondence between our theoretical structure and the overall pattern of the data. With respect to the aforementioned question, if one suspects that the method will always produce an increase in the observed cases of war diffusion under the treatment condition, see table 3.9 where failure does occur.

baseline cases. Even colonial borders (B3) and ententes (A3), the weakest of the individual effects, produce significant increases on war joining when combined with the other variables, and, indeed, even when combined with each other (178 percent).

Given the various combinations of our variables, it is, of course, difficult to produce an ordered prediction of their strength as we did with the single variables. However, it is worth noting that when the class of the WBN is held constant and the alliance class varies, with one exception the magnitudes of the impact are ordered within the groups. The sole exception is that the combination of contiguous WBNs is only marginally stronger with entente WAPs (413 percent) than it is with neutrality WAPs (404 percent).

Thus far our consideration of the problem of war diffusion has treated all states as if they were the same except for their exposure to the various treatments. Much of international relations theory, however, relies upon the knowledge that all states are not the same. The distinction between nations that are major powers and those that are minor powers has been central to an overwhelming part of the field of international relations. For our purposes,

TABLE 3.5. Effects of Combined Border and Alliance Treatments for All Nations, 1816–1965

| Condition | Cell h Percentage | | Percent Change |
	No Treatment	Treatment	
B1A1	5.1	41.8	+719**
	(N = 755)	(N = 55)	
B1A2	4.4	22.2	+404**
	(N = 204)	(N = 27)	
B1A3	3.6	18.5	+413**
	(N = 211)	(N = 65)	
B2A1	6.8	47.8	+602**
	(N = 355)	(N = 23)	
B2A2	4.5	30.0	+566#
	(N = 112)	(N = 10)	
B2A3	6.4	33.3	+420**
	(N = 250)	(N = 27)	
B3A1	6.5	34.1	+424**
	(N = 352)	(N = 44)	
B3A2	4.8	14.2	+195
	(N = 83)	(N = 14)	
B3A3	5.5	15.3	+178**
	(N = 253)	(N = 72)	

Tests of significance:
Difference of proportions, ** = $p < .01$; Fisher's exact, # = $p < .05$

too, this is an important distinction since there is ample reason to believe that major and minor powers will differ in their behavior with respect to opportunity and willingness in joining wars. Specifically we should expect the major powers to respond to opportunities that are cross-water or colonial because in the first instance they have the greater capabilities necessary to become involved, and in the second instance they not only have the capabilities but are much more likely to have colonial borders. Moreover, while minor powers certainly had many alliances, major powers are overrepresented among the states with alliances, particularly defense agreements.

The previous neatness of the analysis begins to break down when we analyze the data separately for the major and minor powers in the international system. Let us begin with the major powers, shown in table 3.6. The effects of the individual border and alliance conditions for the major powers are given in table 3.6. Here it may be seen that while each of the variables had a discernable effect on war diffusion, the results depart from the magnitudes and orderings given in table 3.4. Cross-water WBNs are the strongest border effect for the major powers, as are neutrality WAPs. As we expect from our ideas about the strength of various forms of opportunity, colonial WBNs have only a weak effect.

Note, however, that generally alliances are of more importance for major powers than borders, and that this relationship is stronger for major powers than for all states combined. By definition, major powers are those actors with

TABLE 3.6. Effects of Individual Border and Alliance Treatments for Major Powers, 1816–1965

Condition	Cell *d* Percentage		Percent Change
	No Treatment	Treatment	
B1	7.2	17.5	+143**
	(*N* = 304)	(*N* = 103)	
B2	7.7	24.4	+216**
	(*N* = 353)	(*N* = 78)	
B3	9.4	17.9	+90**
	(*N* = 256)	(*N* = 123)	
A1	9.9	40.0	+304**
	(*N* = 191)	(*N* = 40)	
A2	5.9	27.3	+362#
	(*N* = 67)	(*N* = 11)	
A3	10.2	26.5	+159**
	(*N* = 137)	(*N* = 49)	

Tests of significance:
Difference of proportions, ** = $p < .01$; Fisher's exact # = $p < .05$

global (or at least multiregional) interests and capabilities. And, as major powers, they would be more likely to be able to dominate smaller neighbors. As such, the greater impact of alliances is not surprising.

Table 3.7 presents the combinations of variables for the major powers. Again, there is clear interaction involved in these combinations, some of them astonishingly large; indeed *every* individual condition improves with the combined effects of borders and alliances. The combination of colonial WBNs and neutrality WAPs, for example, produces an increase over the baseline of 813 percent. As might be suspected in the case of such a sharp increase, the number of cases is small: $N = 3$. Similarly, the cross-water WBNs and neutrality WAPs produce a gain of 1,019 percent for four cases.

More surprising, perhaps, than the size of some of the gains observed is the fact that the combination that previously demonstrated the largest gain, the combination of contiguous WBN and defense WAP, for the major powers shows only a modest increase. Here the gain is only 302 percent; and while such an increase is not to be ignored, its modest size relative to some of the other combinations of variables is not in accord with what we would expect

TABLE 3.7. Effects of Combined Border and Alliance Treatments for Major Powers, 1816–1965

Condition	Cell h Percentage		Percent Change
	No Treatment	Treatment	
B1A1	9.2	37.0	+302**
	($N = 152$)	($N = 27$)	
B1A2	5.9	40.0	+577#
	($N = 67$)	($N = 5$)	
B1A3	9.5	30.8	+224
	($N = 105$)	($N = 26$)	
B2A1	10.6	61.1	+476##
	($N = 161$)	($N = 18$)	
B2A2	6.7	75.0	+1,019##
	($N = 60$)	($N = 4$)	
B2A3	10.9	64.3	+489##
	($N = 128$)	($N = 14$)	
B3A1	15.1	70.0	+363##
	($N = 106$)	($N = 20$)	
B3A2	7.3	66.7	+813#
	($N = 41$)	($N = 3$)	
B3A3	11.8	40.0	+238**
	($N = 102$)	($N = 25$)	

Tests of significance:
Difference of proportions, ** = $p < .01$; Fisher's exact, # = $p < .05$, ## = $p < .01$

from our interpretation of opportunity and willingness or the findings already presented. The significant increase found in the effects of B3, colonial borders, in combination with all alliance types may be related to the Starr and Most (1978) findings on the relationship between colonial borders and war. In the 1946–65 period, the strongest relationship between number and type of borders and war participation occurred with borders generated by colonial possessions. The results were even more striking when limited to only the five major powers. In the present study, while the *N*s are rather small, it is clear that the combined effects of colonial borders *and* alliances—(far-flung) opportunity and willingness—now match the earlier findings and arguments about the interests and capabilities of major powers. These findings give us some anticipation about what will be found with the minor powers, to which we now turn.

Table 3.8 reports the individual effects of WBNs and WAPs for the minor powers. First, it may be noted that with two glaring exceptions—B2 and B3, where the increases are very low—the treatment variables had clear effects. The strongest of these was the presence of defense WAPs, where the increase was 451 percent. In addition, the results are ordered as our discussion of the strength of the various indicators suggests. Comparing the results for major powers (table 3.6) and minor powers, the latter are more strongly affected *both* by contiguous borders (B1) and defense pacts (A1). The first finding is expected. Minor powers, virtually by definition, are those with local or re-

TABLE 3.8. Effects of Individual Border and Alliance Treatments for Minor Powers, 1816–1965

| Condition | Cell *d* Percentage | | Percent Change |
	No Treatment	Treatment	
B1	1.9	7.3	+284**
	(N = 2,996)	(N = 669)	
B2	1.9	3.7	+94
	(N = 1,343)	(N = 217)	
B3	1.6	2.8	+75*
	(N = 1,736)	(N = 536)	
A1	3.9	21.5	+451**
	(N = 617)	(N = 65)	
A2	3.6	13.8	+283
	(N = 138)	(N = 29)	
A3	1.6	4.5	+181**
	(N = 316)	(N = 111)	

Tests of significance:
Difference of proportions, * = $p < .05$, ** = $p < .01$

gional concerns. Given the limited capability and ability of minor powers to project power, and thus their greater concern with viability in terms of immediate neighbors, direct borders should be of greatest importance.

The A1 results, however, are more intriguing. As discussed earlier, previous work by Siverson and King (1979) has demonstrated that alliances are likely agents of diffusion. Such research results directly address the war-alliance relationship of concern to many scholars, and the related assertion that alliances act as *conduits* for the spread of international conflict (e.g., see Starr 1978b). Alliances might bring great power conflict into the regional subsystems of small allies; conversely, alliances might drag major power allies into the local conflicts of their smaller alliance partners. Since the bulk of minor power defensive alliances are with major powers, the A1 results appear to indicate in which direction the alliance conflict conduit has tended to work—minor powers being pulled into the ongoing wars of their major power allies. This would appear, for instance, to be the case for most of the medium and small power Western participants in the Korean War; or the group of U.S. allies that assisted America in the Indochina conflict.

Table 3.9 reports the results of the nine combinations of variables for the minor powers. Again, some of the increases are, to say the least, sharp. The situation where we expect the largest increase, contiguous WBNs and defense WAPs, does indeed show the strongest increase, with a magnitude of over 1,000 percent. Moreover, this time the number of cases is *not* small. The first three variable combinations all show marked increases, then something interesting takes place.

Once the *more distant* forms of opportunity and willingness are encountered, the results drop substantially. In fact, for the last six combinations in the table, the results are either meager or nonexistent. For all of these cases, the combined treatment results are *less* than the effects of the individual treatments; that is, the combined conditions make war diffusion less likely. For the first time the results show *negative interaction*. One may initially suspect that this result is nothing more than the artifact of variable combinations producing numbers of cases so small that they disappear. But, as shown in table 3.9, this is not the case. While the number of cases does go down because of the combination, the numbers are certainly sufficient that the absence of an effect cannot simply be attributed to that artifact.

The more likely explanation is to be found in the fact that these combinations do indeed represent the more distant forms of opportunity and lesser types of willingness and that minor powers, because of their lesser capabilities, are either reluctant or unable to enter conflict. Wars, after all, do impose costs on participants, and minor powers may not be in positions where the costs are tolerable.

TABLE 3.9. Effects of Combined Border and Alliance Treatments for Minor Powers, 1816–1965

| Condition | Cell h Percentage | | Percent Change |
	No Treatment	Treatment	
B1A1	3.9	46.4	+1,089**
	(N = 603)	(N = 28)	
B1A2	3.6	18.2	+405**
	(N = 137)	(N = 22)	
B1A3	1.6	10.2	+537**
	(N = 306)	(N = 39)	
B2A1	3.6	0	−100
	(N = 194)	(N = 5)	
B2A2	1.9	0	−100
	(N = 52)	(N = 6)	
B2A3	1.6	0	−100
	(N = 122)	(N = 13)	
B3A1	2.8	4.2	+50
	(N = 246)	(N = 24)	
B3A2	2.4	0	−100
	(N = 42)	(N = 11)	
B3A3	1.3	2.1	+61
	(N = 151)	(N = 47)	

Test of significance:
Difference of proportions, ** = $p < .01$

Are There Possible Uncontrolled Effects from the Research Design?

Anyone who is familiar with research design in those areas where experimental controls are more common may look at the results given in tables 3.4 through 3.9 and have a question about how pure the effects identified really are. For example, in table 3.4 we note a gain of 262 percent over the baseline for a warring contiguous border nations. Strictly speaking, it is not possible to make this claim since the cases affected by the warring border nation effect may also have been affected by any one of the alliance variables or even one of the other border variables. Because we have not controlled for the possible effects of the other variables, some of the apparent effect of a warring contiguous border nation could, for example, be due to the presence of a defense alliance. This is, in some respects, similar to the problem of multicollinearity in regression analysis.

Our ability to investigate this possibility directly is somewhat limited since a full research design allowing the necessary controls and incorporating all the possible interactions is subject to the same constraints that prohibited the use of log-linear methods—a table of vastly greater proportions than the number of cases available for analysis will permit. Specifically, a full consideration of all the individual and multiple effects would generate a table of over 700 cells.

While such a task does not appear desirable, there is a way of gaining insight into whether there may be joint effects in the data. The first step we take is to examine the correlation matrix among all the independent variables for the cases in which war diffusion took place. Table 3.10 shows the results of this procedure. What would be of concern in table 3.10 would be the appearance of a large number of strong positive correlations among the independent variables. Instead, only two statistically significant ($p < .05$) positive relationships may be found. A nation's number of warring colonial borders is moderately associated with both its number of warring cross-water bordering nations (.27) and the number of its warring defense alliance partners (.26). While these two results are statistically significant, their magnitude is not particularly large. Although our overall conclusion is that not much of a problem exists, we need to address directly the magnitude of the effect of the two variables just identifed as correlated with warring colonial borders. Table 3.11 shows the baseline and treatments for the effects of warring colonial

TABLE 3.10. Pearson Correlations among Independent Variables

	Direct	Cross-water	Colonial	Ally1	Ally2
Cross-water	−0.192				
Colonial	−0.385**	0.277**			
Ally1	0.165	−0.086	0.260*		
Ally2	0.102	0.118	−0.132	0.004	
Ally3	0.052	0.080	0.121	−0.079	−0.102

$N = 90$
$* = p < .05$
$** = p < .01$

TABLE 3.11. The Effects of B3 when B1 and B2 Are Absent

	Baseline	Treatment	Percent Difference
Colonial	1.16	2.01	+73.3
	($N = 172$)	($N = 397$)	

$p > .20$ = not significant

borders when no warring cross-water borders or warring defense allies are present. This analysis shows us that indeed the correlated variables were responsible for some of the warring colonial border effects shown in table 3.4. But note that without the presence of the two correlated variables, warring colonial borders still have a 73.3 percent effect, which is, as before, the weakest effect present.

We can carry this investigation one step further by looking at the possibility that the very strong effects of alliances shown in table 3.4 is responsible for some degree of the border effects in that table. In other words, since alliances, and defense alliances in particular, seem to have the strongest overall effects, what happens to the border effects when no alliances are present? Table 3.12 displays the results of tabulating the border data in all those cases in which a warring alliance partner of any kind was *not* present. From this it may be seen that the impact of all types of borders drops. However, two things need to be observed about the nature of this decrease. First, the effects, although less than those originally observed, are in each case still appreciable. Note, for example, that the weakest relationship, that for colonial borders, still shows an increase of 76 percent over the baseline. Second, the magnitude of the increases remains in the same order we originally observed, and it is that which was suggested in our earlier discussion of opportunity.

Before moving on there is a final aspect of the data in table 3.10 that deserves comment. Some may find it curious that the correlations shown in table 3.10 reveal an interaction between any of the variables that are clearly shown to combine with powerful effects in tables 3.5, 3.7, and 3.9. Consider, for example, the combination of warring contiguous borders and warring defense alliance partners: In table 3.10 these two variables show a correlation

TABLE 3.12.   The Effects of B1–B3 when Nations with WAPs Are Absent

Border	Baseline	Treatment	Percent Difference
B_1	1.5 (2,169)	5.1 (641)	+240**
B_2	2.1 (1,137)	4.5 (243)	+114*
B_3	1.7 (1,434)	3.0 (542)	+76*

* = $p < .05$
** = $p < .01$

of only .165, but in table 3.5 they combine to increase the chances of war diffusion by more than 700 percent over the baseline. Why do they show such a strong apparent interaction with respect to war diffusion, but such a low bivariate correlation with each other? This is an important question because it leads to an answer that is both conceptually and substantively quite significant. The answer is to be found in the fact that the data in table 3.10 reflect the correlations for all ninety-four cases of war diffusion, but the effect shown in table 3.5 is based upon their joint occurrence in twenty-three of the ninety-four instances of war diffusion. In essence, they do not occur together in most cases of war diffusion; but *when* they do, there is a strong effect, which is the essence of our argument and not an artifact of the data or the analysis.

A Problem?

Before drawing the results together there is a problem, or puzzle, that must be addressed. Throughout the data analysis it may be seen that there is a consistent pattern wherein the number of nations exposed to the various treatments is very large relative to the number of nations that actually join the war. Consider, for example, the data in the bottom section of table 3.1, which offer the clearest display of this pattern. The data in that table show 1,421 cases of nations exposed to any of the treatments but only 86 instances of the exposure result in the nations joining a war. To be sure, the proportion of those joining under the treatment is considerably larger than under the baseline, but it is nonetheless perplexing that only 6.44 percent of the cases exposed to any form of the treatment joined a war. We have raised this question earlier, but it deserves some amplification here.

There are a number of possible approaches to evaluating the impact of these error cases to the validity of our findings. First, recall that earlier we explicitly stated that we are working within a framework of loose necessity. Under this circumstance we expect that there will be many error cases, but that such error is more apparent than real. The requirements of opportunity and willingness predict not that a state exposed to these conditions will join a war but only that its probability of joining will be substantially higher than where those conditions are not present. This situation is quite similar to that encountered by Bueno de Mesquita (1981) in his consideration of the initiation of war. In his analysis it may be seen that states have positive expected utility for war far more than they actually go to war, while in this research there are far more WBN-WAP interaction opportunities than there are instances of diffusion.

In this research the importance of the idea of necessity may be seen in figure 3.1. The concern with overprediction is reflected in the number of cases in cell *b*. However, for necessary relationships the number of cases in *b* is irrelevant. The relevant cell to compare to cell *d* is *c*, which should be empty. Given our loose necessity formulation, we should expect only a few cases in *c*, especially as a percentage of the total number of cases in the no treatment column (i.e., the *a* + *c* column). Returning to table 3.1, it is clear that although there are a very large number of cases in the no treatment column (2,328), there are only 8 in cell *c*. Similar relationships occur in the matrices that provide most of our results; in the example given in note 9 reporting the results of contiguous WBNs there are only 27 cases in *c* out of a possible 2,977 cases.

There is a second way to investigate the error cases. It is instructive to examine once again the data in table 3.2. There it may be seen that most of the error is to be found in those cases in which a nation was exposed to only one of the treatments; the 703 error cases under that condition represent 52.7 percent of the total error. As exposure goes up, the rate of war joining goes up quite sharply. The question now is whether or not the 712 cases (i.e., the 703 cases of error and the 9 cases of war joining) that received only single treatments are distributed evenly across the opportunity and willingness variables. Table 3.13 summarizes this distribution. Clearly, exposure to a single B1 or B3 happened fairly frequently but did not have much of an effect.

In terms of the epidemiological analogy for the diffusion process, there is a most interesting implication that may be drawn from these observations: Decisions to join an ongoing war face considerable friction. Earlier we spoke of conditions that could act as barriers to diffusion, or, in Rapoport's terminology, that limit the spread of disease. One of the limiting conditions Rapoport (1960, 52) mentions is the "virulence" of the "pathogenic organism." We have now identified a crucial aspect of the virulence of borders and alliances as agents of diffusion—the number of treatments to which states are exposed. A single opportunity is rarely associated with war joining. It is only when the opportunities begin to accumulate, or, more importantly, are attached to the

TABLE 3.13. Occurrence of Single Border and Alliance Treatments, All Nations, 1816–1965

Variable	Number of Single Treatments	Percent of Total
B1	328	46
B2	75	10.5
B3	259	36.4
A1	10	1.4
A2	6	0.8
A3	34	4.8

political affinity indicated by an alliance that the chances of joining an ongoing war begin to build significantly.

The fact that wars are, in a sense, undersubscribed is not surprising. Theories of collective goods and the free rider tell us that it is not rational for nations to undertake a costly course of action if someone else will do it for them (Olson and Zeckhauser 1966) and wars can be among the most costly of all the courses of action nations may choose. Thus, the costs of war may also be seen as a limiting factor. While abundant opportunities exist, willingness is required for joining an ongoing war. Such willingness is more likely to be present the more virulent the diffusion situation—the larger the number of exposures in a state's environment.

Conclusion

This chapter began with the aim of investigating the diffusion of war, in terms of the expansion of ongoing conflict, between 1816 and 1965. This was done in the context of opportunity and willingness, as indicated by warring border nations and warring alliance partners. We have proposed a relatively simple expectation derived from the opportunity, willingness, and interaction opportunity concepts and investigated it through a set of comparisons between treatment and nontreatment groups of data. The data presented in the tables in this chapter support the contention that war does expand among states along the indicators that operationalize opportunity and willingness and that the strength of the relationship is ordered by the type of border or alliance, as hypothesized.

We have added to the understanding of war diffusion in several ways. While one body of previous research has indicated an important geographic basis for diffusion, and other research has indicated that alliances are important in spreading conflict, this work (based on the synthesis noted in chap. 2) has the virtue of *combining* geographic and political variables so that the strong interaction of these two elements may be observed.

The scope of this analysis is also more extensive than previous studies of war diffusion. The data used are global (and not limited to any single geographic region) and cover all international wars from 1816 to 1965.[12] We

---

12. The Altfeld and Bueno de Mesquita (1979) data are much more limited because they are interested only in those cases of war expansion that took place within the first two months of a war. Hence, their main data set contains only 40 cases of war joining. In addition, they exclude from their data set the participation of the four Commonwealth nations (i.e., Canada, Australia, New Zealand, and South Africa) that joined World War II in 1939 on the grounds of missing data; that is they had no alliance memberships. Those cases are included here. We also include the cases from the Korean War, which were totally excluded by Altfeld and Bueno de Mesquita; see their note 7 (94).

provide separate analyses of major and minor powers, revealing different patterns of diffusion and indicating how major and minor powers differentially relate to the elements of opportunity and willingness.

Perhaps most useful to the theoretical development of the study of war diffusion, we have more evidence as to the applicability of research based on opportunity, willingness, and their interaction.[13] We have more confidence in the theoretical scope of this approach in that we now find that it can help explain two different conceptualizations of diffusion: (1) the emulation, or linkage-penetration view taken in earlier research, where events elsewhere change a state's disposition to behave similarly; and (2) an infection-contagion approach taken in this chapter, where diffusion is conceived of as the growth of ongoing wars.

The refinement of such analytic tools is vital in the design of future research. With multiple sources of evidence indicating that diffusion processes of various kinds do exist in international relations, we now require further work in the specification of the *processes* at work in various kinds of diffusion, including the conditions under which the diffusion of violent conflict takes place. The further specification of these processes might also help us understand the interaction between opportunity and willingness and various theories of why wars at particular times are more likely to be larger than at others.

---

13. In this chapter, we have shown that this theoretical approach is applicable to large-scale war as delineated by the Correlates of War Project's data set. The previous applications of this approach by Most and Starr, as noted, were dominated by violent conflict of a smaller scale, whether internal or external.

CHAPTER 4

The Problem of Time in the Diffusion of War

The analyses in chapter 3 have been undertaken within a context of geopolitical considerations in which war diffusion takes place across *space* through the interaction of various opportunities, indicated by various levels of geographic proximity, coupled with differing amounts of willingness, evidenced by various alliance commitments. Here we turn to an exploration of the impact of opportunity and willingness on the *time* that elapses between the onset of a war between two nations, say N_1 and N_2, and the entry of other nations $N_3. \ldots . N_i$. That is, we are now focusing on what we described in chapter 2 as the "time-space convergence" (Hagerstrand 1967).

Even a cursory examination of the historical facts reveals that while some nations appear to become involved in a war quickly, others take a considerable period of time to make their choice. For example, on July 16, 1870, France declared war on Prussia; within the next few days, Wuerttemburg, Baden, and Bavaria joined the war on the Prussian side against France in what would become the Franco-Prussian War. Although those nations joined the war relatively quickly, in World War II Italy waited until more than nine months after the initial hostilities to enter the war. Our central question in this chapter is to what extent do opportunity and willingness explain such variation?

The Data

The first task in our problem is a determination of the unit of time in which diffusion will be measured. This unit needs to meet at least two criteria: (1) it should be as precise as possible, and (2) we should have high confidence in its accuracy. The need for precision is, of course, based upon the desire to have a measurement that will furnish as much information as possible. However, this information and its precision would be illusory if we did not have a high degree of confidence in its accuracy. With this in mind, we chose as our measure of time the number of days that elapsed between the onset of a war and the time various other nations beyond the first two joined the ongoing war. Gradations finer than this are not generally available and would likely not be generally reliable, while turning to a coarser measure would throw away information. The data collected by Small and Singer are recorded by the day the war begins as well as by the day each nation joined. A review of their data indicates that they are fairly reliable, and only a few dates of entry were recalculated. For example, we noted that Prussia's allies among the German states were recorded as joining the Franco-Prussian War on July 19, 1870, at the same time as France and Prussia. Other sources, including contemporaneous newspaper accounts, give the dates of their joining as one to two days later.[1]

In most respects the generation of the data now appears to be fairly easy. In most ways this is true in that it is necessary only to identify the nations joining a war and measure the number of days that passed between the outbreak of the war and a nation's participation. Most such information is readily available in Small and Singer's data. There is, however, one aspect of the research question that leads us to make one minor modification in the simple procedure just outlined.[2]

World Wars I and II are world wars only when seen *post facto*. Put differently, to a considerable extent they represent whole events only when seen from the vantage point of history. As these conflicts developed, at the *time of their occurrence* they may be seen as a series of unfolding wars, led in general by the calculations of the major powers (Yamamoto and Bremer 1980). In this respect it is reasonable to measure the time between a nation's entry and the last previous new participation in that war by a major power. Thus the time of Mongolia's 1945 entry into World War II is measured not from the date of Germany's attack on Poland but from the date of the Soviet Union's entry into the war against Japan.[3]

Also we need to note that in one important respect the data may have the

---

1. See, in particular, the *Times* (London) for July 19–22, 1870. In reviewing the manner in which various data sets treat the time of war entry, we not only encountered the relatively modest error in the Singer-Small data for the entry of the German states into the Franco-Prussian War but also noted a major error in Wright's (1965, 1,537) report of Bulgaria's declaring war on the United States in World War II on June 22, 1941, six months before Pearl Harbor; the actual date for this should have been December 13, 1941.

2. We eliminated some cases of war joining listed by Small and Singer. For those cases in which nations joined a war and then changed sides (e.g., Bulgaria, Hungary, and Italy in World War II), we include in the data only their first participation. We also eliminated China and Japan as joining World War II on December 7, 1941. Those nations had been at war since the middle of 1937 and while it is probably correct to merge them into World War II in December, 1941, it seems inadvisable for us to include them in our data as war joiners, although we do include the United States as joining the war in December, 1941.

3. Four cases were removed from the ninety-four cases analyzed in the previous chapter. We removed China and Japan as joining World War II on December 1, 1941, since they had been fighting since 1937. Having them join the war, as in the sense of the previous chapter was justified, but in terms of elapsed days, it seems contrived. We also removed Australia and New Zealand from World War II, since they were missing data on all variables.

appearance of lacking homogeneity. What we mean by this is that it is not possible for all cases to take any of the observed values of the time variable. While Italy joined World War II on June 10, 1940 (283 days after the German attack on Poland), it was not possible for a nation to have joined the Seven Weeks War after the same amount of time had elapsed because by that time the war was over. Joining the Six Day War of June, 1967, was even more difficult. One solution to such a problem is to divide each war into its early, middle, and late stages. However, when a war starts, decision makers do not know when it will end; beyond the beginning, they do not *know* the point at which they are entering a war. Not infrequently initial expectations that a war will be short are incorrect; witness, for example, the cases of World War I and the Vietnam War. While nations are certainly aware of joining a war at its beginning, after any reasonable amount of time has passed, they cannot be certain of whether they are joining in the middle or at the end, although many decision makers may have the expectation that they are joining at the end, as witness Mussolini's decision to join World War II.

We also need to recognize that not all nations join a war in the same manner. In 1939 Britain declared war against Germany after Germany attacked Poland. Germany did not attack Britain. In this sense the British had what we will call some *latitude for decision*. Without an attack on Britain by the Germans it was necessary for the British to take the initiative. On the other hand, after the German invasion in 1940 Norway had only the choice of resisting or not. It does not necessarily make sense to treat such cases as equivalent. War takes a decision by two nations: one to attack and the other to resist.[4] Consequently, we coded our cases into those states that had not been attacked and had relatively high decision latitude and those that, having themselves been attacked, had relatively less.[5]

---

4. It should be pointed out that not all nations resist. Denmark did not resist the German invasion, nor in 1939 did the Baltic republics resist the Soviets.

5. This requirement for a dyadic conception of war—where *two* or more states are willing and able to pursue hostilities—is discussed in Most and Starr (1989, chap. 4) and is crucial to the definition and conceptualization of war. Delineating which country was the initiator and which the target was usually fairly clear. However, the entry of the United States into World War I gave us some difficulty. America's entry followed the German decision for and declaration of unrestricted submarine warfare. The Germans may have been daring the United States to enter the war, but it was a dare that left some choice with the United States. Because of this we coded the United States as having decision latitude, but recognize that some may reasonably differ with that choice.

We introduce the idea of decision latitude here and not in the last chapter because when those data are analyzed using decision latitude as an additional variable, two things happen. First, under several of the border-alliance conditions there are either no cases or too few to be useful. When there are a sufficient number of cases, no statistically significant differences appear.

Data Analysis

In the analyses in chapter 3, we have used an approach based upon something close to a quasi-experimental design. However, because the variable we wish to explain here, elapsed time, is continuous, we can approach this analysis within the framework of regression. An initial difficulty with this, however, is the distribution of the elapsed time variable. As shown in figure 4.1, the data have a rather peculiar distribution. They are strongly skewed (skewness = 2.257) to the left and also have a very high variance. In fact, the mean of the elapsed time is 203.4 days with a standard deviation of 356.2. This is not a very satisfactory situation, but it is not beyond solution. A log transformation of the data reduces the amount of skewness a substantial amount (skewness = 0.261, mean = 2.7, SD = 2.4). In addition, the use of the log transformation has substantive implications since it squeezes the data together and thus reduces their heterogeneity.

Our independent variables are the same as those used in chapter 3, except that instead of examining the effects of the presence or absence of warring border nations (WBN) or warring alliance partners (WAP) we will explore the effects of a nation's *number* of WBNs or WAPs on the elapsed time that it takes that nation to become involved in the war. Thus our independent variables are counts of the number of occurrences for each treatment variable used in chapter 3.[6]

An Initial Analysis

Within the logic of the interaction opportunity model is the assumption that states with greater interaction (through borders or alliances) have greater importance and salience to each other. In this chapter we are looking at those states that *do have* either WBNs or WAPs and that *did* enter a war through a diffusion process. The interaction opportunity model would lead us to expect that if bordering states or alliance partners become involved in war, then the greater importance of those countries and thus the greater uncertainty of the environment generated by their being at war should lead those at peace to a greater willingness to participate in that war. Hence, we are led to the hypothesis that the greater a nation's opportunities and willingness, the *less* time it will take that nation to become involved in the war. The degree of opportunity or willingness is operationalized through the different types of borders and the different types of alliance ties that states might have with one another.

---

6. Tufte (1974) recommends a log transformation of all variables that, like our independent variables, are counts. Our variables, however, have a sufficiently normal distribution that the transformed results do not differ appreciably from the raw data.

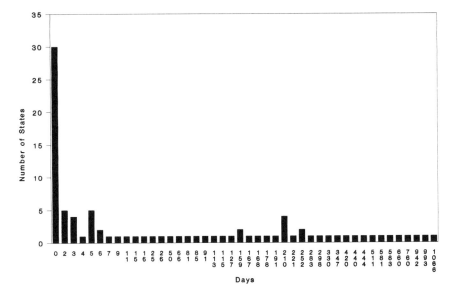

Fig. 4.1. Distribution of time elapsing from war onset to war entry, by states

Table 4.1 reports the results of regressing the elapsed time variable on the three opportunity and three willingness variables. Under our general expectations we anticipate finding that the variables would be ordered in such a way with respect to elapsed time that both B1 and A1 would show the strongest

TABLE 4.1.   Regression of Elapsed Time on Opportunity and Willingness

Variable	Coefficient	SE	Standard Coefficient	Tolerance	t	p(2 tail)
Constant	3.544	0.562	0.000		6.309	0.000
B1	−1.028	0.494	−0.231	0.7530583	−2.081	0.041
B2	−0.686	0.717	−0.105	0.7730554	−0.958	0.341
B3	1.206	0.509	0.286	0.6400132	2.370	0.020
A1	−0.588	0.452	−0.134	0.8730223	−1.300	0.197
A2	1.263	0.727	0.173	0.9415743	1.738	0.086
A3	−1.368	0.615	−0.226	0.8998761	−2.223	0.029

Variance	R^2	df	$\bar{R}$	F-ratio	p
Regression	125.787	6	20.964	4.069	0.001
Residual	427.628	83	5.152		

Dep Var: DAYSLOG; N = 90; Multiple R = .477; R^2 = .227; Adjusted R^2 = .171; SEE = 2.270

negative relationships, followed by B2 and A2, and then by positive relationships between time and B3 and A3. The results in table 4.1 are generally consistent with these expectations. The standardized coefficients for B1 (−.23) and for B2 (−.10) indicate that as nations had more direct and cross-water borders they tended to enter the war sooner, while those that had colonial borders entered the war later (B3 = .286). The results for the alliance variables are not so neat, for while the number of defense alliances was negatively related to time, the A2 and A3 variables are both stronger and in the reversed order, .185 and −.228, respectively. However, while the overall results are statistically significant ($F = 4.069$; $df = 6$ and 83, $p = <.001$), the individual variables reveal that only three (B1, B2, and A3) are significant beyond .05.

Recall the distinction we drew between those nations that had high decision latitude in entering a war and those whose latitude was more limited in that they had been attacked by someone else and had the choice only of capitulation or war. As we suggested, it is not unreasonable to expect that these two groups of nations may have been differentially affected by opportunity and willingness and that they should be examined separately. Table 4.2 reports the regression results for the opportunity and willingness variables for those nations with high decision latitude. Since this is a fairly large proportion of our data (seventy of ninety cases), the standardized coefficients are very similar to those from the previous table in their direction and magnitude. The alliance data, once again, are not ordered the way we expect them to be, with defense alliances (A1) appearing to lengthen the amount of time for diffusion

TABLE 4.2. Regression of Elapsed Time on Opportunity and Willingness, Nations with High Decision Latitude

Variable	Coefficient	SE	Standard Coefficient	Tolerance	t	p(2 tail)
Constant	3.674	0.575	0.000		6.390	0.000
B1	−1.421	0.560	−0.327	0.7311386	−2.539	0.014
B2	−1.025	0.771	−0.162	0.8093299	−1.329	0.189
B3	0.729	0.563	0.187	0.5824130	1.295	0.200
A1	0.263	0.572	0.059	0.7479771	0.461	0.647
A2	−0.369	0.921	−0.044	0.9810040	−0.400	0.690
A3	−1.072	0.629	−0.205	0.8386754	−1.703	0.093

Variance	R^2	df	$\overline{R}$	F-ratio	p
Regression	91.890	6	15.315	3.278	0.007
Residual	294.336	63	4.672		

Dep Var: DAYSLOG; $N = 70$; Multiple $R = .488$; $R^2 = .238$; Adjusted $R^2 = .165$; SEE = 2.161

and the position of the other two variables again reversed. It is, however, noteworthy that the results for B1 remain relatively strong (and statistically significant) and the overall analysis of variance is significant ($F = 3.278$, $df =$ 6 and 63, $p = .007$).

When we move to the analysis of the low decision latitude cases, as shown in table 4.3, the results reveal a very interesting twist. For the first time the alliance variables are ordered in the predicted direction and A1 and A2 constitute the only significant relationships in the table. The overall regression has an adjusted R^2 of .460 and the overall results are significant.

A Smaller Model

Since we are interested in trying to formulate the most parsimonious model, we should try to examine the most significant relationships in the two previous analyses and include the effects of decision latitude within the regression. Table 4.4 reports the results. As we would expect from the previous analyses, the number of warring, directly bordering nations is the strongest influence on elapsed time and offers by itself a reasonable fit. However, neither the number of warring defense partners nor decision latitude achieves statistical significance, although the latter comes fairly close.

Given these findings, we need to examine the possibility that there is interaction in the data between defensive alliances and decision latitude. Table 4.5 reports the results of including this interaction term in the regression with B1. The changes in the results are rather dramatic. The standardized coeffi-

TABLE 4.3. Regression of Elapsed Time on Opportunity and Willingness, Nations with Low Decision Latitude

Variable	Coefficient	SE	Standard Coefficient	Tolerance	t	p(2 tail)
Constant	6.138	1.846	0.000		3.326	0.005
B1	−1.209	1.121	−0.212	0.7129343	−1.079	0.300
B2	−3.361	1.824	−0.469	0.4277053	−1.842	0.088
B3	0.959	1.492	0.177	0.3638580	0.643	0.531
A1	−2.828	1.115	−0.660	0.4089634	−2.537	0.025
A2	3.353	1.193	0.561	0.6939636	2.810	0.015
A3	1.595	3.350	0.084	0.8927610	0.476	0.642

Variance	R^2	df	$\bar{R}$	F-ratio	p
Regression	105.765	6	17.627	3.855	0.020
Residual	59.440	13	4.572		

Dep Var: DAYSLOG; $N = 20$; Multiple R: .800; $R^2 = .640$; Adjusted $R^2 = .474$; SEE $= 2.138$

TABLE 4.4. Regression of Elapsed Time on Opportunity, Willingness, and Decision Latitude

Variable	Coefficient	SE	Standard Coefficient	Tolerance	t	p(2 tail)
Constant	6.092	1.307	0.000		4.662	0.000
DIRECT	−0.735	0.199	−0.395	0.8641979	−3.701	0.000
A1	−0.234	0.447	−0.053	0.9452611	−0.523	0.602
DECSLT	−1.198	0.632	−0.201	0.8784358	−1.896	0.061

Variance	R^2	df	$\bar{R}$	F-ratio	p
Regression	83.979	3	27.993	5.128	0.003
Residual	469.436	86	5.459		

Dep Var: DAYNEWL; N = 90; Multiple R: .390; R^2 = .152; Adjusted R^2 = .122; SEE = 2.336

cient for borders remains about the same as that shown in the previous table, but the number of warring defense alliance partners becomes more important as does the interaction between defense alliances and decision latitude. In fact, even decision latitude by itself is more important than borders.[7]

A Different Analysis

In order to show these results somewhat more clearly, we will now move our analysis away from the regressions and back toward an approach similar to that used in the main part of chapter 3. The main elements of the model shown in table 4.4 may be analyzed in tabular form by examining the time it took for the various individual nations to become involved in a war under a variety of conditions: (1) neither an A1 or a B1 is present; (2) an A1 is present, but a B1 is not; (3) an A1 is absent, but a B1 is present; and (4) both an A1 and a B1 are present. To measure the time it took for diffusion under these conditions, we use the median number of days from war onset to war involvement. It is, of

---

7. At this point it might be asked why the analyses shown in this chapter (particularly the analysis shown in table 4.4) do not report a comparison of the baseline and treatment conditions as was done in chapter 3. The answer to this is that such a comparison is not possible. In chapter 3 the comparison was between nations that joined a war and those that did not. Here all the nations joined; there is no set of baseline nations. A second approach might be to compare the effects of the treatment variables, such as warring defense alliances nations, to those same variables that are not treatments, such as a nation's total number of defense alliances. This would, of course, reveal that the same variation would be captured by the baseline as by the treatment because the two variables are so highly correlated; that is, a nation with many allies is, other things being equal, more likely to have more of them in the war and, more importantly, a nation with few allies cannot have many warring allies. A baseline comparison, in short, makes neither substantive nor methodological sense.

course, tempting to use the mean number of days, but given the skewed distribution shown in figure 4.1, the results would not be nearly as meaningful as with the median.

Table 4.6 shows the results for the overall relationship between the presence or absence of a defense alliance, the presence or absence of a warring border nation, and the median number of days to war involvement of those that joined. This table gives a slightly different description of the relationships between B1 and A1 and the median elapsed time variable. As might be expected, the median elapsed time is greatest (115 days) when both B1 and A1 are absent. On the other hand, the median elapsed time is least (2 days) when both A1 and B1 are present. However, it is important to note that when A1 is absent, the effect of B1 is much stronger (5 days) than the effect of A1 when B1 is absent (66 days). Moreover, note also that there are 50 percent

TABLE 4.5. Regression of Elapsed Time on Opportunity, Willingness, and Interactive Term

Variable	Coefficient	SE	Standard Coefficient	Tolerance	t	p(2 tail)
Constant	8.676	1.516	0.000		5.723	0.000
B1	−1.554	0.451	−0.350	0.8774854	−3.444	0.001
A1	−4.876	1.597	−1.114	0.0679552	−3.053	0.003
DECSLT	−2.597	0.778	−0.435	0.5319976	−3.338	0.001
A1* DECSLT	2.728	0.912	1.075	0.0701750	2.993	0.004

Variance	R^2	df	$\overline{R}$	F-ratio	p
Regression	127.671	4	31.918	6.372	0.000
Residual	425.744	85	5.009		

Dep Var: DAYSLOG; $N = 90$; Multiple R: .480; $R^2 = .231$; Adjusted $R^2 = .194$; SEE = 2.238

TABLE 4.6. Mean Elapsed Time to War Entry by Warring Defense Alliance Partner and Warring Direct Border Nation

	Defense Alliance		
Direct Border	No	Yes	
No	115	66	100
	($N = 15$)	($N = 9$)	($N = 24$)
Yes	5.0	2.0	3.5
	($N = 33$)	($N = 33$)	($N = 66$)
	8.0	3.0	5.5
	($N = 48$)	($N = 42$)	($N = 90$)

more cases when B1 is present than when A1 is present, with forty-two versus sixty-six cases, respectively. This suggests that to some degree the regression findings in table 4.4 may be due to the simple fact that in a world in which most nations have borders and only a minority have defensive alliances, there were simply more warring border nations than warring defensive alliance nations.

Diagnostics

Before interpreting these findings, it is appropriate to check the results of our regressions to determine the extent to which the findings may be influenced by unrecognized problems in the analysis, such as collinearity, hetero-scedasticity, or distorting effect being given to the regression because of the impact of outliers.

Collinearity does not appear to be a problem. Each of the regression tables reports the tolerance of the individual variables. Tolerance is one minus the squared multiple correlation between each independent variable and the remaining independent variables in the equation. As collinearity increases, tolerance moves toward zero. All the relationships we have examined have fairly high scores for tolerance except where interaction is introduced in table 4.5. Since by definition interaction terms must be collinear in some way, it is not surprising to find it. The more interesting question, of course, is whether it distorts the analysis. That it does not is indicated by the fact that, despite collinearity, the t ratios remain high (Lewis-Beck 1980).

Figures 4.2 and 4.3 display the normal probability plots of the residuals from tables 4.1 and 4.5, respectively. As may readily be seen, each is fairly consistent with the straight line that follows from the desired condition of a normal distribution of the residuals.

In checking the regression for outliers, we found that for the regression in table 4.5 two cases have relatively high leverage.[8] We eliminated these cases (Baden and Wuerttemburg in the Austro-Prussian War) from the data set and ran the same equation against the reduced data set. Only minor differences were found between these results and those obtained originally.

Although it is not part of the diagnostics, there is another aspect of the data and the findings that emerge from them that merits investigation. To some degree the speed of diffusion is reliant upon the speed with which people find out about some event. Obviously, it is not possible for a nation to join a

---

8. Leverage is an index of the magnitude of the effect of each case on the size of the mean square error. According to Velleman and Welsch (1981) leverage should have an average value of p/N, where p is the number of parameters to be estimated and N is the number of cases. When leverage is in the range of $2p/N$, there is probably an undue effect in the observation.

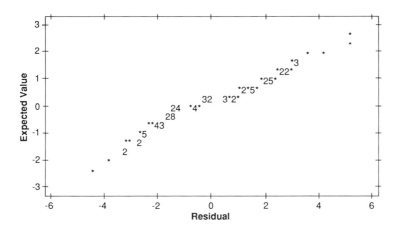

Fig. 4.2. Normal probability plot of the residuals from table 4.1

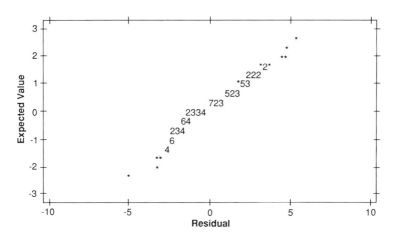

Fig. 4.3. Normal probability plot of the residuals from table 4.5

war before it knows that the war is taking place. As noted in chapter 2, technology is an important mechanism for overcoming the constraints of distance and topographical barriers. The speed of communication has increased rapidly over time, and so it might be reasonable to expect that the elapsed time it takes a nation to join a war might be influenced at least to some degree by improvements in communication technology over time. To what extent is this the case? Do nations join wars more quickly as improvements in communication have taken place? The answer is easy to find by regressing the elapsed time variable on the year in which the war took place, making the not unreasonable assumption that progress in communication technology at least approximates linearity.

The regression results shown in table 4.7 demonstrate a moderate relationship between the year a war started and elapsed time that passed between a war's onset and the nation's involvement, but this relationship is in the *opposite* direction from what the communication hypothesis predicts. Instead of decreasing with the passage of time, elapsed time has tended to increase over the years. One interpretation of this is that as war has become more deadly and potentially more costly to nations, decision makers have become somewhat more cautious about committing their nations to war.

Certainly, war has at least been perceived as becoming more deadly and costly. The reluctance of the British and French to become militarily involved with Germany despite Hitler's series of aggressive actions in the 1930s is a prominent pre–World War II example. In the postwar era, the existence of nuclear weapons and the perceptions of their destructive power may also be cited as an example of costs encouraging caution on the part of decision makers (the most recent versions of what actually occurred during the Cuban missile crisis strongly support this hypothesis; see, for example, Garthoff 1989). While there are a number of ways to interpret the data on war-generated casualties, it is clear that the two world wars occurring in the first half of this century were in terms of the sheer number of battle deaths the two deadliest violent conflicts since the inception of the Westphalian state system in the middle of the seventeenth century (see Levy 1983; Richardson 1960.).

Nevertheless, looking at the data collected by the Correlates of War Project on the relationship between the year a war started and its severity, as measured by battle deaths, provides scant evidence that more recent wars have higher casualties (Small and Singer 1982, 138, table 7.6,); in fact, we find only a relatively weak correlation (.11) between the two variables, one that is not statistically significant. This relationship seems to run against the widely

TABLE 4.7.   Regression of War Year and Elapsed Time

Variable	Coefficient	SE	Standard Coefficient	Tolerance	t	p(2 tail)
Constant	-38.715	13.893	0.000		-2.787	0.007
Year	0.022	0.007	0.303	.100E+01	2.982	0.004

Variance	R^2	df	$\bar{R}$	F-ratio	p
Regression	50.781	1	50.781	8.891	0.004
Residual	502.634	88	5.712		

Dep Var: DAYNEWL; $N = 90$; Multiple R: .303; $R^2 = .092$; Adjusted $R^2 = .081$; SEE = 2.390

held belief that more recent wars have been more severe. One of the explanations Small and Singer advance for this belief (141–42) is that the increasing technology of communication (which might be said to begin with Mathew Brady's photographs of the American Civil War) brings home the slaughter of war in a manner that is difficult to ignore. If true, this could imply that the effect of improved communication is not, as we originally suspected, a device to speed the spread of war but one that may deter the willingness of nations because the costs of war participation are being better appreciated.[9]

Discussion and Conclusions

What conclusions may be drawn from this analysis? The first and most simple conclusion is that the relationship between opportunity and willingness and the time of war entry is a complex one. Although the set of straightforward hypotheses linking opportunity and willingness to the time frame within which nations will join ongoing conflicts is broadly supported by the analysis in table 4.1, the subsequent analyses reveal more interesting and more complicated relationships.

By looking at the decision latitude of nations, we can differentiate rather clearly between the impact of our indicators of opportunity (borders) and willingness (alliances) on the time elapsing before diffusion takes place. Where decision latitude is high, where states at peace have not themselves been directly attacked by one of the participants in an ongoing war (table 4.2), borders and opportunity have the primary effect on the timing of new war entries. These results conform to the logic of the interaction opportunity model as outlined by Most and Starr (1980) in their discussion of borders and geographic proximity: war in bordering states may significantly alter the levels of salience, concern, and uncertainty in states still at peace but bordering on those that are at war. This logic was confirmed in studying the relationship between borders and war (for example, see Starr and Most 1978; Siverson and Starr 1988) and borders in the diffusion of war. The closer a state is to a war, and adding the first law of geography, i.e., the principle of least effort, to proximity, we have also found that states bordering a war with high decision latitude will more quickly join that war than those nations that are more distant.

For states that enjoy high decision latitude, the opportunity provided by borders appears to be more important than the willingness of alliances. Without the stimulus of an attack, which characterizes low decision latitude, the alliance factor remains open. That is, without the immediacy produced by an

---

9. Part of Mueller's (1989) argument that modern war has become obsolescent is related to the fact that citizens have more information about its true horror.

attack and the salience generated by borders, whether or not a state's alliance commitments will bring it into war alongside its partners rests upon the whole array of diplomacy and bargaining games that affect any decision to go to war, or the foreign policy of a state in general. From table 4.2 it may be seen that there is no clear pattern to the presumed strength of alliance commitments or warring alliance partners and the timing of war entry.

We have used alliances as surrogates for a broad conception of willingness. The timing of the willingness to enter an ongoing war under conditions of high decision latitude are quite complex and are addressed across a range of works in the international relations literature. One specific line of relevant inquiry is Bueno de Mesquita's treatment of expected utility and whether or not alliances will increase or decrease willingness to fight and under what conditions willingness is most likely to be increased (Bueno de Mesquita 1981; Altfeld and Bueno de Mesquita 1979; Bueno de Mesquita and Lalman 1986). Some might argue that whether or not alliance ties will speed a third party into an ongoing war would rest on a variety of calculations. These would include the costs and benefits of opposing a would-be hegemonic power or alliance, or balancing, as against the alternative of joining what is perceived to be the ultimately victorious side, or bandwagoning (Walt 1985; Garnham 1988). States might also attempt to calculate which side in an ongoing conflict would provide greater postwar payoffs (Starr 1972); that is, which would best offset the costs of war with the benefits of being on a winning side? Related to this is the collective good payoff of simply being on the winning side (again, see Starr 1972)—and thus the calculations of the power of each side, and how such calculations affected projections of victory and defeat. States might also consider questions such as who was the initiator and who was attacked to calculate the odds of victory and/or to raise considerations of domestic support for joining one side or the other.

Factors such as these are basic to the calculation of utility and ultimately willingness—both the willingness to enter a war at all (as all the states under study in this chapter did) and the timing of such an entry. Without a direct attack, and thus with high decision latitude, these factors come into play in such a way that the warring alliance partner variable by itself is inadequate.

Given the array of factors such as those just noted, we can only speculate on the anomalous effect of ententes (A3) shown in table 4.2. Recall that the manner in which the types of alliances scaled changed when looking at countries with different levels of decision latitude. When we investigated states with *high* decision latitude, ententes had the strongest effects, *lowering* the time in which states with entente ties joined ongoing wars. While not statistically significant, defense alliances (A1) produced a result that indicated that they *increased* the time taken to enter a war. However, when looking at states with *low* decision latitude, ententes produced no effects, while the results for defense pacts were significant and in the right direction (that is, decreasing the time in which defense alliance partners entered a war).

Several interpretations, based on the nature of the alliance experience, suggest themselves. One possible point worth making is that allies with weak alliance ties might want to prove themselves in some way to their partners and enter the war earlier than otherwise indicated. This would be consistent with participation models of coalition payoff distribution discussed by Starr (1972). In contrast, when there is low decision latitude, that is, when a state has been the subject of an attack by some other nation, the calculations change. A state may resist or not resist. As indicated in table 4.3, states are more likely to resist if their alliance partners are already involved. This is most clearly the case with defense pact partners (A1) and less so with other types of alliance partners. Given that such an attack has *already taken place*, the factors that make contiguity so important under high decision latitude are now moot. Thus, as shown in table 4.3, under such circumstances borders tend to make little difference.

Our results may also rest on basic differences between the nature of ententes and the nature of defensive alliances. Kann (1976), in an essay looking at the different relationships that ententes and alliances (which we have termed *defensive alliances,* A1) might have with the outbreak of war, focuses his discussion on the rigidity of the different types of agreements. He compares the effectiveness of alliances that are "rigidly" defined to "more flexible associations between states such as ententes, nonaggression pacts or consultation pacts . . . " (611). The arguments that he develops rest on this comparison between rigid versus loose or flexible agreements; alliances involving stronger commitments (such as coming to the partner's aid, or, to a lesser degree, not attacking the partner) compared to the weaker commitments of ententes that involve consultation.

A key to Kann's discussion, as well as interpretation of our results, is the definition or operationalization of *entente*. The Correlates of War definition, which we have employed, rests on the concept of *consultation*. However, Kann (1976, 611) goes beyond this conceptualization: "The concept of entente, taken from the Franco-British Entente Cordiale of 1904 and made more specific in 1912, is usually referred to as the classical case of a flexible agreement of cooperation between two sovereign powers. By intent far more loosely defined than an alliance, 'entente' is a more meaningful term than 'consultation' or 'nonaggression pact.' In many instances, either of the latter may serve the same purpose as an entente."

In a commentary on Kann, Berridge (1989, 252) concurs with this approach based on flexibility in a strong critique of the Correlates of War definition of entente (see also Levy 1981:587–88). Differences in the flexibility or rigidity of alliance arrangements permit us to put our results in a broader context. Kann (1976, 612) argues:

> It seems fair to say that, exceptions notwithstanding, an alliance with rigid commitments leads to an attitude in which each state tries to minimize its own obligations and to maximize those of its partners. Consequently, in most alliances there exists a built-in centrifugal tendency toward weakening the ties—a trend found throughout the history of alliance systems. . . .
>
> Where no firm commitments exist between the partners, there should be simple recognition of the fact that agreements between them will make sense only if they serve common interests. Assuming mutual reasonableness to be the raison d'etre of accords, one can argue that the *partners of an entente or consultation pact will be interested in strengthening their ties* [emphasis added].

This logic matches up exactly with the results reported in Tables 4.2 and 4.3. With high decision latitude, entente partners would be concerned with "strengthening their ties" and entering a war more quickly, not out of a rigid, and perhaps artificial, set of alliance commitments that might be less relevant than when originally formulated. Perhaps one useful example of this would be pre–World War I Japan seeking acceptance and status in the Eurocentric international system. Having concluded ententes with France and Russia in 1907, Japan entered the war only three weeks after France did.

With high decision latitude, defense pact partners would still be seeking to minimize their obligations. However, under conditions of low decision latitude—that is, being attacked—alliance partners would be seeking to *maximize* the obligations of their alliance partners. This would best be done by joining a war quickly and demonstrating important contributions to the war effort, a point that is also argued by Starr's (1972) findings on war coalition behavior.[10]

As indicated in our opening chapters, we have used alliances in this study as a surrogate for *willingness*. The investigation of the speed with which alliance partners enter an ongoing conflict exemplifies this use of alliances, looking not at opportunity or even interaction opportunity but at alliance as a conscious policy choice, which sets the stage for a series of conscious policy choices.

---

10. We should note, too, that the rigidity of alliances is seen by both Kann and Berridge as advantageous to alliance partners in situations characterized by a strong reliance on deterrence (e.g., Berridge 1989, 254–55). See also our discussion in chapter 2.

Before closing, several points must be made clear. As noted in chapter 1, the diffusion of war is not a highly frequent occurrence in international conflict, given the total number of wars that have taken place. In the research reported here we have looked only at those states that have been involved in one form of diffusion, entry into an ongoing war. Among these states, most enter an ongoing war under the condition of high decision latitude. Thus in investigating factors affecting the length of time taken to enter an ongoing war, *opportunity* in the form of shared borders appears to be the most fruitful avenue of inquiry. As noted, a full study of willingness in terms of the speed with which states enter wars requires a more detailed look at the variety of factors affecting the utility of such a decision.

CHAPTER 5

Explicating Opportunity, Willingness, and the Diffusion of War

In a recent collection of empirical studies on war, the editors pose a crucial task (Gochman and Sabrosky 1990b, 5): "Since war is a reality of our time and place, we need to ask whether we are, perforce, prisoners of war." This question has many facets. It is a newer version of the older adage that to do something about war we need to understand it. The primary concern with understanding war has been with its onset—what causes war. It is instructive (and illustrative of the literature) that, of the fourteen analytic chapters in the Gochman and Sabrosky (1990a) volume, the first ten are devoted to the onset of conflict and war. They are followed by only *two* studies on war expansion (Most et al. 1990; Yamamoto 1990). What we have argued in this book is that the expansion of war is an important question in terms of consequences for the participants and the international system. It is an important question for insuring that we think in terms of a conflict *process*. It is an important question for directing attention to the processes of escalation, processes that occur not only in the conflict helix (to use Rummel's term) prior to the outbreak of war, or to the efforts of the original participants, but after a war has started with regard to new participants. Are we prisoners of the escalation and spread of war?

Diffusion and War: So What?

In pursuing the current research project, we have attempted to contribute to the substantive as well as the conceptual understanding of this question. As introduced in the first chapter, the application of diffusion analyses in the context of opportunity and willingness permitted us to bring into focus a perspective that is not common to the study of war, the consequences of war for war. To be interested in the consequences of war for war, then, is to be concerned with what happens after a war begins. The concept of war diffusion has been employed here to indicate that war may have discernible, patterned effects on the international environment and the behavior of the entities within that environment. Starr (1990, 6) has noted: "In this broad sense diffusion can be, and in this study will be, employed as a conceptual or theoretical basis for empirical analysis. That is, diffusion, and methods developed to study it, involves a set of assumptions about the nature of systems, how units interact, and expectations of how the environmental context will affect the behavior of environed units."

On this basis, understanding the consequences of war for war in terms of diffusion requires a broader theoretical view (following Most and Starr 1989). That broader view was provided by studying the diffusion of war within a clearly specified geopolitical context. The *meaning* of opportunity, of alliances, and even of war itself rests upon the theoretical context within which such concepts are studied. Using the work of the Sprouts as a core, a geopolitical context encompassing the constraints and opportunities of time and space was presented. Opportunity and willingness were employed to summarize and synthesize the various components of a Sprout-based geopolitical perspective. Only after a clear understanding of possibilism and cognitive behaviorism could a diffusion approach based on opportunity and willingness be pursued.

Within such a theoretical context, diffusion provided us with a handle on how war may systematically affect the international system and the consequent war behavior of its members. Despite a wide variety of forms and definitions, at its heart, "Diffusion refers to the process by which institutions, practices, behaviors, or norms are transmitted between individuals, and/or between social systems" (Welsh 1984, 3). Thus, in the first two chapters we outlined the concept of diffusion employed in our research—diffusion as infection—and how it could be studied employing the interaction opportunity model. The research design needed to apply this model was introduced and elaborated upon in chapters 3 and 4.

Research Findings

The *substantive* questions concerning diffusion were presented at the beginning of the first chapter: (1) can we identify the necessary conditions for war diffusion; and (2) can we use these conditions to understand the speed with which states are likely to join a war after it has begun? Our answers to these questions were presented in chapters 3 and 4. These answers contribute significantly to the *additive cumulation* occurring in the study of war diffusion and geopolitics.[1] They provide further evidence that there is systematic diffusion of international conflict, and that it can be modeled and studied.

Very simply, we were able to demonstrate in chapter 3 that borders and

---

1. See Zinnes (1976), as well as Most and Starr (1989), for discussions of the nature of cumulation. A special issue of *International Interactions* (vol. 17, nos. 1–2) provides some idea of both the additive and integrative cumulation occurring in this subfield.

alliances create the salience and/or the ease of interaction (as predicted by the interaction opportunity model) that significantly increases the probability that states will join ongoing wars. Both bordering states that were at war and alliance partners that were at war increased the probability that states at peace would become war participants. The effects of different types of borders were ordered as predicted by the idea of opportunity; the effects of different types of alliances were ordered as predicted by the idea of willingness. In addition to providing support for the pretheoretic opportunity and willingness construct, demonstrating that the border and alliance categories ordered *correctly* was central to developing the hypotheses and discussion in chapter 4 on the timing of war entry.

The analyses in chapter 3 also indicated the existence of important interactive effects between borders and alliances (again, as predicted by the interaction opportunity model). In general the combined effects of warring border nations and warring alliance partners were stronger than either alone. Thus, these analyses also confirmed the use of a *loose necessity* design, by indicating that just one WAP or WBN treatment was often not enough to produce a diffusion effect. Some combination of WBN and WAP effects, as well as multiple treatments, appears to be required to overcome the conditions limiting the spread of the *war disease,* to overcome the barriers to diffusion. In addition, the fact that interactive effects were uncovered reinforces the conception of geopolitics we have employed. The interactive effects found derive from the combination of spatial or geographic factors and political ones—a combination of opportunity and willingness.

However, as noted in this book and demonstrated in Most and Starr (1989), the relationship between opportunity and willingness is a complex one. Where the concept of diffusion across *space,* broadly viewed, was the central question addressed in chapter 3, diffusion across *time* was the central question addressed in chapter 4. Again, the interaction opportunity model as operationalized through borders and alliances could account for the speed with which states joined ongoing wars. It is interesting to note that over and above the interactive effects found, we could say that alliances had a greater impact on the spatial dimension of diffusion while borders had a greater impact on the time element. In terms of the initial process by which states decide to join wars, it appears that *willingness* (for which alliances acted as a surrogate) had the greater effect. Given whatever impact opportunity (operationalized through borders or proximity) had at this first stage, it appears that opportunity had the greater effect on the timing of entry into ongoing war.

These empirical findings, while useful, are only part of the story. They have raised, once again, the question of the relationship between opportunity, willingness, and the choice to enter into war. The "So what?" question has a theoretical side as well. At this point we are now able to say additional things about a set of theoretic and conceptual tools—the opportunity and willingness framework, geopolitical models, and an epidemiological metaphor. The place of willingness in the choice of alliances and war can now be elaborated. It is to these concerns we now turn.

Opportunity/Willingness and War

We have also tried to add significantly to *integrative cumulation* in the study of war. For Zinnes, integrative cumulation means that a new study "ties together and *explains a set* of research findings," going beyond earlier studies (Zinnes 1976, 162, emphasis in original). In this study the elaboration of opportunity and willingness as geopolitical and decisional components of diffusion models is directed toward cumulation in the study of war and alliance, diffusion models, and the evolution of opportunity and willingness from a pretheoretic form to a full-fledged theory.

The notion that the phenomenon of war, as exemplary of other forms of interdependent outcomes, is dependent upon the jointly necessary conditions of opportunity and willingness has been reconfirmed and extended. One way we have done this is by indicating the success of the interaction opportunity model for the study of infectious diffusion, for both major powers and the full international system, and, in contrast to the post–World War II period examined in earlier studies, across a significant span of international history

The requirement of both opportunity and willingness for increasing the probability of joining ongoing war also helps to explain war as a relatively rare event and justifies the use of the epidemiological metaphor. Perhaps more important is the further evidence that opportunity and willingness have complex interactive effects of their own in establishing the geopolitical context that any state and its decision makers face at any point in time.

Borders, warring border nations, and the more general set of geopolitical factors in the environment, especially alliances, provide a *structure* of opportunities and constraints (as argued in chap. 2).[2] Recall, however, that structure is more than simply opportunity or possibilism. Structure also involves the presentation of an array of risks and opportunities to decision makers. Opportunity was conceived as consisting of both the possibilities that exist in the international system at any point in time as well as how those possibilities *were distributed* among the actors in the system.

The possibilities or opportunities that exist, along with their distribution, help us understand how costly or risky certain options appear to decision makers, and how the decision makers might calculate willingness to act. That is, the geopolitical structure of opportunities and constraints (possibilism) are

---

2. These ideas are also elaborated in Starr (1991).

translated through environmental probabilism into the incentive structures of human beings who have to make choices. The geopolitical environment, then, has an impact on both opportunity and willingness, as people perceive the environmental opportunities and constraints (cognitive behaviorism), plug them into a structure of incentives that make choices more or less likely and through some form of utility calculations affect the willingness to behave.

This is the central mechanism of the interaction opportunity model. The salience of having a bordering nation at war, *plus* the ease of military interaction that is increased by proximity, is a central feature of the geopolitical structure or context that any state faces. Salience can also be demonstrated through alliance ties. Alliance membership comprises part of the *political* component of *geopolitics*, based on willingness to ally with states on the basis of common policy objectives. In addition to presenting a full outline of the interaction opportunity model, the analyses presented in this book also confirmed the utility of the interaction opportunity approach through the empirical analysis of infectious diffusion.

The combination of possibilism, probabilism, and cognitive behaviorism, empirically tested within a loose necessity framework, is additionally important in laying to rest any potential claims of geopolitical determinism. The rareness of war and war diffusion requires a nondeterministic theory and methodology. Geography and geopolitical factors matter, but only in nondeterministic ways.

Most and Starr (1989, 24) note: "At their most basic level opportunity and willingness may be used both to help in partitioning the world, and by organizing our thinking in these terms, to help in bringing disparate phenomena together in an orderly manner." It was argued that opportunity and willingness were particularly useful in organizing material in areas such as international conflict, where important and relevant findings are derived from many disciplines and across all levels of analysis. It was specifically argued that the use of opportunity and willingness was superior to the organization of material on a disciplinary basis, or along levels of analysis (as initially introduced by Waltz [1954]). While a number of studies from the 1970s and 1980s were noted, this argument can be updated using a recent overview of the literature on war (Levy 1989), which is both extensive and insightful but limited by its restriction to a levels-of-analysis approach.

Levy (211–12) identifies the problem correctly when he notes: "In particular, scholars have failed to integrate what we know about individual psychology with what we know about organizational behavior, political economy, and state-society relationships into a theory of how *states* make foreign policies on issues of war and peace." It should be clear to the reader by now that the Sprouts' ecological triad does just this, and that the opportunity and willingness variant is designed specifically to achieve this objective. The theoretic outline in this book, buttressed by empirical findings, indicates how the synthesis Levy calls for can be accomplished. However, while admonishing scholars of international conflict for their lack of synthesis (and after Most and Starr have demonstrated that such a synthesis cannot be achieved by using a levels-of-analysis approach),[3] Levy then concludes, "I have adopted a *levels-of-analysis framework* to classify the independent explanatory variables and in this way to organize our examination of theories of war" (1989, 222, emphasis in original).

This is curious, in part, because a central issue Levy wishes to address is the claim made by some analysts "that the causes of war are eternal, that nothing has changed in the nuclear age . . . , and that consequently their theories are as applicable today as in previous eras" (217). While Levy returns to this theme on several occasions, a satisfying conclusion is never reached. One reason is that simply classifying independent variables by level of analysis will not distinguish the nuclear era from previous historical situations. What are required are studies of willingness, as in the expected utility tradition of Bueno de Mesquita (1981), placed within the changing set of possibilities created by the technology of nuclear weapons and their delivery systems. Any special distinction that may be found in the nuclear era will emerge through the study of willingness given the dynamism of the geopolitical environment.

The problem with using a levels-of-analysis approach to organize findings and theory is similarly illustrated by the difficulty in *locating* work such as Bueno de Mesquita's within the *proper* level (see Levy's footnote 53 [1989, 304]). However one wants to argue over Bueno de Mesquita's operationalization of his model, or what level of analysis that operationalization taps, the model or theory *is about willingness*; it is about incentive structures and how those structures are affected by the geopolitical environment. A puzzlement concerning what to do with the literature on the debate over the effects of polarity (Levy 1989, 235) exhibits the same problem. Indeed, the conclusion to the whole section on systemic factors (262) suffers from the lack of a conceptual bridge to societal and individual decision-making factors (as does the conclusion to the section on misperception [288–89] but in the other direction). Without the jointly necessary concepts of opportunity and willingness, or any similar scheme, the findings at one level float free without logical links to others.

Especially in contrast to overviews of war based on levels of analysis (or disciplinary organization), we hope we have indicated the value of the opportunity and willingness framework—how it forces the analyst to take a holistic

---

3. Note that the Most and Starr (1989) material was strongly based on arguments made by Starr (1978a) over a decade earlier and raised in their series of earlier articles.

perspective; how it facilitates the inclusion of environmental and contextual factors back into our analyses; how it can help provide meaning to otherwise free-floating concepts (as illustrated by the treatment of alliances in this book).

Willingness: The Alliance-War Nexus

In focusing on the consequences of war for war, and the application of opportunity and willingness to the study of war diffusion, we have also paid particular attention to alliances in international relations. Alliances have been demonstrated to be an important part of the geopolitical context of states, and from this perspective the salience of alliance partners has been explicated. The salience of alliance partners, in turn, indicates the utility of investigating WAPs in the study of diffusion. Alliances have also been used as a surrogate for willingness, as a conscious policy choice of states (see chap. 2).

Two central aspects of willingness have been raised in this study. One, as just noted, is the willingness to enter alliances. The other is the willingness to join ongoing wars. *Why* do foreign policy decision makers choose to join a conflict that is in progress? If opportunity and willingness are useful in bringing disparate phenomena together in an orderly manner as we have asserted, perhaps the opportunity and willingness framework can be of use in demonstrating that these two seemingly separate questions of willingness are, indeed, related.

In discussing probability models directed toward explaining the growth of war coalitions, Yamamoto (1990, 233) similarly notes: "Since one of the major characteristics of war expansion is the number of belligerent nations in a war and since the process of war alliance formation is conceived in these probability models as one in which alliances acquire new belligerent members, I use the terms *war expansion* and *wartime alliance formation* interchangeably" (emphasis in original). Thus, in Yamamoto's context, infectious diffusion can be discussed interchangeably with the growth of war coalitions.

In chapter 2 we indicated that the question of entering an alliance is a complex one, based on calculations of cost and benefit. While declining to go into why states join alliances in depth, we outlined briefly the major costs involved in alliance: being called upon to support one's allies, particularly by going to war. We noted that such costs needed to be weighed against benefits in some form of expected utility calculus. In a study of the relationship between alliance and war, Wayman (1990, 111) characterizes alliances in analogous utility terms: "In this sense, alliances, like weaponry, are a form of risk taking. They trade off a little more war proneness, which is bad, for a little greater chance of victory, which is good for your side when . . . victory is meaningful." More simply, Yamamoto (1990, 237) asserts "The basic assumption in the rationality model developed here is that nations initiate, or enter belatedly into, a war because they see more benefits than costs in their actions."

The application of utility models to the question of why states join alliances, and especially why states enter war coalitions, is important because a utility perspective also forms a basis for the interaction opportunity model. Yamamoto (1990) is concerned with the expansion of war and contrasts what he sees as two competing approaches, probability models and rationality models. Again, we believe that we can demonstrate that the interaction opportunity model of diffusion based upon opportunity and willingness can be used to bridge both approaches.

Interaction Opportunity and Utility Calculations

Returning to the arguments developed in the opening two chapters, we begin with the assertion that the existence of war in the international system changes the context within which the actors of that system must operate. The analyses presented in chapter 4 indicating the impact of decision latitude support this assertion. The interaction opportunity model posits, however, that those effects are differentiated. In any system that exhibits interdependence, activity (such as war) in some part of the system will have an impact on all members of the system. Nevertheless there are factors that increase the *sensitivity* of states to the effects of war. These factors, of course, include the salience and ease of interaction that form the core of the interaction opportunity model.

Salience and ease of interaction affect willingness through the impact they have on the incentive structures and cost-benefit calculations of decision makers. Both borders and alliances, as noted, create a structure of risks and opportunities. This idea was derived from work mentioned and discussed more fully throughout this book. Midlarsky (1975) raised the issue of uncertainty—that larger number of bordering states increased uncertainty through lesser control over the environment and that states would be willing to go to war to reduce that uncertainty.

The interaction opportunity model additionally argues that such uncertainty would be exacerbated by the presence of war on bordering territory. Insecurity would be heightened.[4] One reason for heightened insecurity has been addressed in the work of Diehl (1987, 1988), which looks at territory in terms of the stakes involved. Neighboring states are more likely to come into conflict over contending claims to territory and are also more likely to lose

---

4. Insecurity has also been linked to contiguity through Converse's (1968) "control paradigm": the inability to control neighboring states and/or the fear of coming under their control, either of which can lead to aggression.

territory to each other. Diehl notes that some issues have greater importance than others, namely, greater stakes. Territory is such an issue (as also demonstrated in terms of territorial payoffs and losses after war by Starr [1972]). As such, territorial issues appear to generate greater insecurity and intensity of reaction (e.g., for joining a war).

The link between uncertainty, insecurity, and threat was partially raised in our earlier discussion of Walt's (1985) framework regarding the reasons states join alliances. We agreed with Walt that *threat* was the key to the decision whether or not to balance or bandwagon. Such threat could be clearly linked to ideas by Boulding that we raised earlier—security (and insecurity) defined in terms of viability; and viability as a function of distance through the loss-of-strength gradient. While borders, as a measure of proximity, are clearly relevant to threat or viability, we presented a discussion indicating how alliances produced similar consequences.

The threat and uncertainty produced by neighboring states at war or by alliance partners at war may be transformed into a decision to join that war. There are a variety of ways by which this could happen. Two simple scenarios indicate the types of utility calculations that could take place.

1. Suppose that State *A* is made conditionally viable in its homeland by State *B*. State *A* might resent this situation but be hopelessly unable to do anything to alter it. If State *B* becomes involved in a conflict with some third state, *C*, however, the strength of *B* at *A*'s homeland might be reduced to the point where *A* could take advantage of the opening provided by *B*'s commitment of its strength against *C*, and launch an attack of its own.

This case, then, involves an ongoing war leading to new participants through an attack on a belligerent that is perceived to be weakened through the war or at least perceived to have had its military capability spread thin or made unavailable. The option of joining the war has now been made to look attractive to an initially weaker state (*A*) through the effects of war on an initially stronger state (*B*). Some of this logic is implicit in Paul Kennedy's (1987) extensive discussion of the rise and fall of the great European powers (again, see especially his sections on the Habsburgs).

2. Suppose that *A* and *B* are both unconditionally viable (that is, secure) and that *B* is waging a war against a third state, *C*. If the leaders of *A* perceive that *B* is winning the conflict, and that as a consequence it might be in a position to make *A* only conditionally viable, then State *A* may launch an attack of its own to help defeat *B*, or simply to protect its own position.

In essence this scenario is a form of what Walt calls "balancing." Here, a state's (B) involvement in war appears to make that state *stronger*, and in preemptive fashion other states (such as A) enter the war to stop B before it actually does achieve the strength to threaten A's viability.

These scenarios are not exhaustive, of course, and could be discussed at much greater length. They do help to illustrate the consequences of war (and especially bordering war) on perceptions of threat and calculations of security, cost, and benefit. Indeed, if it is the case that borders and alliances create a structure of risks and opportunities, the fact that a bordering state or an alliance partner is at war redefines the situation and opens up *new risks and opportunities*. It is this new structure that provides the setting for new war participation or infectious diffusion.

Probability and Rationality Models

As noted earlier in this section, Yamamoto set out to contrast models of the growth of war coalitions based upon assumptions rooted in probability theory with those based upon assumptions of rationality. The rationality model is based on a relatively simple cost-benefit calculation (1990, 237–38): "If decision makers see more benefits than costs and if the net benefit of nonparticipation is zero, they will enter into the war; otherwise they will not. Suppose that a war is in progress. If some of the nonparticipating nations see more benefits than costs associated with becoming belligerents, at least one of the contending alliances will acquire new members and become larger. However, if none of the nonparticipants sees more benefits than costs, the alliances will not acquire any new members and will therefore cease expanding."

A key phrase above is "if none of the nonparticipants sees more benefits than costs." Looking at baseline data presented in chapter 3, we see that just about every country has borders and/or alliance partners. Thus, the chances are that states at war will *be* WBNs or WAPS to some set of nonparticipating third parties. This set of third party states will have more salient and crucial calculations to make. These third party states will be more likely to see benefits to their threat or viability situation by entering the war. As we have demonstrated, the states in this set will do so more often than those not bordering and/or allied to belligerents.

One of Yamamoto's key assumptions for the rationality model is that "the cost and benefit functions are the same for all nonparticipants in a particular war . . . that every nonparticipant has the same parameter values for a particular war" (1990, 238, 246). The most important feature of the interaction opportunity model, and one supported by the empirical research reported in this book, is that the cost and benefit functions *are NOT the same for all nonparticipants*. The baseline analyses in chapter 3 clearly demonstrated this point. The utility calculations of nonbelligerents is significantly affected by differential contexts in terms of what we have called *treatments*. The presence of a WBN and/or a WAP increases the utility of joining the war.

Based on the important probability model of the expansion of war coalitions developed by Horvath and Foster (1963), Yamamoto derives a set of assumptions that underlie a stochastic model of war coalition growth. The logic of the central assumption of the probability model is in part supported by our work, but in the main is also called into question. Yamamoto (1990, 233) presents the central assumption as follows:

> The larger the alliance, the greater the probability that it will acquire new members. This implies that the probability that each nonparticipating nation will join the alliance increases as the alliance becomes larger. This is the most important assumption in the model in the sense that it stipulates that war expansion is a self-aggravating process. The larger a war becomes, the more likely it is that the war will continue to expand.

Indeed, as each war becomes larger, the web of relevant borders and alliance contacts becomes more extensive. Thus, the probability that the war will continue growing does increase. However, the probability model *does not* specify the mechanisms by which war will expand and thus does not address the question of limits—how and why does a war *stop* growing? Because the interaction opportunity model of diffusion does specify the process of expansion, it can also indicate—theoretically and empirically—what the barriers to diffusion are.

Our findings concerning the impact of multiple treatments or interactive border or alliance treatments are important in this context. Wars do not simply follow a process of unending growth. There are limits to epidemics. The perceived expected utility from entering war that triggers willingness is neither automatic nor easily developed. Thus, Yamamoto's aforementioned comment on the rationality model is relevant here: "However, if none of the nonparticipants sees more benefits than costs, the alliances will not acquire any new members and will therefore cease expanding." Note that the interaction opportunity model is inclusive of this observation and, moreover, provides a fuller explanation for why this is so.

The issue of expansion is illustrative of the incompleteness of the contending models as presented by Yamamoto. Examples may be found in Yamamoto's table 15.4 (1990, 253), which sets out a comparison between the assumptions and results of the probability and rationality models. In regard to alliance behavior, he includes the probability model view: "Wars (war alliances) were homogeneous in expansion. (Every war is the same.)" In contrast, the rationality model asserts: "Wars are not homogeneous. War alliances have different optimal sizes depending on the cost-benefit structure." From the interaction opportunity or diffusion view wars cannot be seen as homogeneous. The interaction opportunity or diffusion model thus agrees with the rationality model but also provides substantive mechanisms that affect the utility calculations. The cost-benefit structure is based on differential geopolitical factors—the presence or absence of WBNs and/or WAPs.

If one looks closely at the probability model, as outlined by Yamamoto, it is seen to draw almost entirely from structural features and statistical possibilities in the system. It is based on opportunity. The rationality model in all its aspects is clearly based on willingness. Once again, for a full analysis that is logically complete as well as empirically verifiable, both opportunity and willingness must be taken into account.

Responding to the "So what?" question has led us to touch on a variety of topics. On the theoretical or conceptual level we have indicated several ways in which this study has supported the opportunity and willingness approach. In turn, we have tried to demonstrate the utility of opportunity and willingness as it applies to the study of war and alliances. Our relatively modest research aims on the infectious diffusion of war were accomplished. In addition to providing new empirical analysis that says something about diffusion and the role of borders and alliances in the spread of war once it begins, however, we have provided a broader conceptual context that helps give meaning to such phenomena as war, alliance, and diffusion. It is clear that despite the attention provided in both Most and Starr (1989) and this volume, we have just begun to tap the richness and complexity of opportunity and willingness.

Appendix

This appendix contains the contiguous, cross-water, and colonial borders for the states we identified and enumerated in our basic data set in the period between 1816 and 1965. For each nation, we have supplied the following information: its three letter abbreviation, identification number, and years of membership in the international system (all derived from Small and Singer 1982), the nations on its borders at the time of its initial membership in the system, and an identification of the border group to which it belongs with a 1 indicating a contiguous border, a 2 indicating a cross-water border, and a 3 indicating a colonial border, either contiguous or cross-water. Subsequent entries after the initial date of system membership indicate changes in borders. For example, the entry for the United States shows it as an initial member of the system in 1816 with colonial borders with Spain and Great Britain. In 1831 it gains Mexico (but keeps Spain because of Cuba, a Spanish colony that is across less than 200 miles of water), and in 1867 it adds Russia with the purchase of the Territory of Alaska, which created a colonial border across less than 200 miles of water. In 1959 Alaska became a state and the colonial border with the Soviet Union was upgraded to a cross-water border. The list is symmetrical in that if Belgium is contiguous with France, then France is contiguous with Belgium, or, less obviously, if France has a colonial border with Canada, then Canada has a colonial border with France. Also note that the zones of allied occupation in post–World War II Europe are included as colonial areas.

The data on colonial borders were the most difficult to obtain because of the number and almost unbelievable obscurity of some colonies. We were aided very considerably in this task by Henige's (1970) comprehensive list of colonial governors. This list, which begins with the fifteenth century, identifies all political units that were the colonial possession of some other nation. Finding them in this list then permitted relatively easy location in a historical atlas. For example, unless one is fairly familiar with North American geography and history, the existence of France's islands, St. Pierre and Miquelon, ten miles off the coast of Newfoundland, would not be recorded, and the colonial border between France and Canada would be missed. Even more obscure is the Caribbean island of St. Barthelemy, located in the northern

Lesser Antilles, which was a Swedish colony between 1784 and 1878 (at which time it was sold to France). However, this territory (p. 56) and 411 others are identified by Henige, although not all of these are relevant since many had disappeared as colonies by 1816, the date our data collection begins.[1]

It should be noted that the data do not record more than one border of any type between any two nations. Thus if France and Spain had 2, 3, or *n* colonies that were contiguous, only one such border is recorded. It might have been desirable to record each such point of contact, but our resources were simply not sufficient to carry out a plan of such ambition.

```
002 USA 1816–1965 /3/ UK SPA
      1831 /1/ +MEX
      1867 /3/ +USR
      1898 /3/ +DEN +DOM +JPN +UK +HAI +NTH
      1899 /3/ +GER
      1902 /2/ +CUB
      1906 /2/ −CUB
      1909 /2/ +CUB
      1917 /3/ −DEN
      1919 /3/ −GER
      1920 /1/ +CAN /3/ +PAN
      1945 /3/ +CZE +FRA +ITA +PAN +UK +USR
      1948 /3/ +PRK
      1949 /3/ −PRK
      1954 /3/ +GDR
      1956 /3/ −CZE −FRA −GDR −ITA −UK −USR
      1959 /3/ −USR /2/ +USR

020 CAN 1920–1965 /1/ USA /3/ DEN FRA
      1953 /2/ +DEN /3/ −DEN

040 CUB 1902–1906 /2/ USA HAI DOM MEX /3/ UK USA
040 CUB 1909–1965 /2/ DOM HAI USA MEX /3/ UK USA
      1915 /2/ −HAI
      1934 /2/ +HAI
      1962 /2/ +JAM

041 HAI 1859–1915 /3/ UK SPA
      1887 /1/ +DOM
      1898 /3/ +USA −SPA
```

---

1. Henige's list was helpful in two other respects. First, without it some colonies would still have been very difficult to locate (e.g., the Danish colony of Tranquebar on the southeast Indian coast). Second, upon occasion some colonies changed hands and then changed back again.

```
    1902 /2/ +CUB −USA
    1906 /2/ −CUB /3/+USA
    1909 /2/ +CUB /3/ −USA
041 HAI 1934−1965 /1/ DOM /3/ CUB UK
    1962 /2/ −UK +JAM

042 DOM 1887−1965 /1/ HAI /3/ SPA UK
    1898 /3/ −SPA +USA
    1902 /2/ +CUB
    1906 /2/ −CUB /3/+USA
    1909 /2/ +CUB /3/−USA
    1915 /1/ −HAI
    1934 /1/ +HAI

051 JAM 1962−1965 /2/ CUB HAI

052 TRI 1962−1965 /2/ VEN

070 MEX 1831−1965 /1/ USA /3/ UK SPA USR
    1848 /3/ −USR
    1849 /1/ +GUA
    1898 /3/ −SPA +USA
    1902 /2/ +CUB /3/ −USA
    1906 /2/ −CUB /3/−USA
    1909 /2/ +CUB

090 GUA 1849−1965 /1/ MEX /3/ UK
    1875 +SAL
    1899 +HON

091 HON 1899−1965 /1/ GUA SAL /3/ UK
    1900 /1/ +NIC

092 SAL 1875−1965 /1/ GUA
    1899 /1/ +HON
    1900 /2/ +NIC

093 NIC 1900−1965 /1/ HON /2/ SAL
    1920 /1/ +COS

094 COS 1920−1965 /1/ NIC PAN

095 PAN 1920−1965 /1/ COL COS /3/ USA

100 COL 1831−1965 /1/ BRA /3/ NTH
    1841 /1/ +VEN
```

```
        1854 /1/ +ECU
        1920 /1/ +PAN
        1942 /1/ +PER
        1940 /3/ −NTH
        1945 /3/ +NTH

101 VEN 1841−1965 /1/ COL BRA /3/ UK NTH
        1940 /3/ −NTH
        1945 /3/ +NTH
        1962 /2/ +TRI

130 ECU 1854−1965 /1/ BRA COL PER
        1942 /1/ −BRA

135 PER 1838−1965 /1/ BRA
        1848 /1/ +BOL
        1854 /1/ +ECU
        1884 /1/ +CHI
        1942 /1/ +COL

140 BRA 1826−1965 /3/ FRA UK NTH
        1831 /1/ +COL
        1838 /1/ +PER
        1841 /1/ +VEN +ARG
        1848 /1/ +BOL
        1854 /1/ +ECU
        1882 /1/ +URU
        1896 /1/ +PAR
        1940 /3/ −NTH
        1942 /1/ −ECU /3/ −FRA
        1944 /3/ +FRA
        1945 /3/ +NTH

145 BOL 1848−1965 /1/ BRA PER CHI ARG
        1896 /1/ +PAR

150 PAR 1896−1965 /1/ ARG BRA BOL

155 CHL 1841−1965 /1/ ARG
        1848 /1/ +BOL
        1884 /1/ +PER

160 ARG 1841−1965 /1/ CHI BRA /3/ UK
        1848 /1/ +BOL
        1882 /1/ +URU
        1896 /1/ +PAR
```

165 URU 1882–1965 /1/ BRA ARG

200 UK 1816–1945 /2/ FRA NTH /3/ DEN FRA NTH POR SIC SPA TUR USA
    USR SWD
    1826 /3/ +BRA
    1828 /3/ +GRE
    1830 /2/ +BEL
    1831 /3/ +MEX
    1838 /3/ +HAN
    1841 /3/ +ARG +VEN
    1847 /3/ +MOR
    1849 /3/ +GUA
    1855 /3/ +IRA +EGY
    1859 /3/ +HAI
    1860 /3/ +CHN
    1861 /3/ +ITA −SIC
    1862 /3/ −ITA
    1864 /3/ −GRE −TUR
    1866 /3/ −HAN +GER
    1867 /3/ −USR +USA
    1878 /3/ +GRE −SWD
    1882 /3/ −EGY
    1884 /3/ +GUA +MEX
    1885 /3/ +BEL
    1887 /3/ +DOM +THI
    1890 /3/ −DEN +ITA
    1898 /3/ − SPN +ETH +JPN
    1899 /3/ +HON
    1902 /3/ +CUB
    1906 /3/ −CUB
    1909 /3/ +CUB
    1911 /3/ −MOR
    1915 /3/ −HAI
    1917 /3/ −DEN
    1918 /3/ −GER
    1920 /3/ +AFG +LIB +NEP +SAF
    1922 /2/ +IRE /3/ +IRE
    1926 /3/ +YAR
    1927 /3/ +SAU
    1930 /3/ −JPN
    1932 /3/ +IRQ
    1934 /3/ +HAI
    1937 /3/ +EGY −ETH
    1940 /2/ −BEL −NTH /3/ −NTH
    1941 /3/ +ETH −GRC
    1942 /2/ −FRA /3/ −FRA −ITA

    1944 /2/ +BEL +FRA +NTH /3/ +FRA +ITA
    1945 /3/ +NTH +BEL
    1946 /3/ +JOR +LEB +SYR +YUG
    1948 /3/ −AFG +IND −IRA −NEP +PAK
    1949 /3/ −IND +INS −JOR −LEB −PAK −SYR
    1952 /3/ +LIB
    1954 /3/ +GDR
    1956 /3/ −DEN −GDR +SUD −USA −USR −YUG +MOR
    1957 /3/ −EGY +GHA −LIB
    1958 /3/ +GUI −THI
    1960 /3/ +CON +SEN +SOM +ZAI
    1961 /3/ −GHA −ITA +TAZ
    1962 /3/ −GUI −IRQ −LBR +UGA
    1963 /3/ +MAL −YAR
    1964 /3/ −ETH −INS −SOM −SUD −UGA +ZAM
    1965 /3/ −CON +RHO −TAZ −ZAI

205 IRE 1922−1965 /1/ UK /3/ UK

210 NTH 1816−1940 /1/ FRA GER /2/ UK /3/ UK POR FRA SPA DEN
    1826 /3/ +BRA
    1830 /1/ +BEL −FRA
    1831 /3/ +COL
    1838 /1/ +HAN
    1841 /3/ +VEN
    1850 /3/ −DEN
    1866 /1/ −HAN
    1884 /3/ +GER
    1898 /3/ +USA −SPA
    1914 /3/ −GER
    1920 /3/ +AUL

210 NTH 1945−1965 /1/ BEL /2/DEN UK /3/AUL BRA COL VEN UK USA
    1955 /1/ +GFR
    1964 /3/ −AUL

211 BEL 1830−1940 /1/ NTH FRA GER /2/ UK
    1885 /3/ +FRA +GER +POR +UK
    1918 /3/ −GER
    1920 /1/ +LUX
211 BEL 1945−1965 /1/ FRA LUX NTH /2/ UK /3/ EGY POR UK
    1955 /1/ +GFR
    1956 /3/ +SUD −EGY
    1961 /3/ −POR −SUD

212 LUX 1920−1940 /1/ GER FRA BEL

212 LUX 1944–1965 /1/ FRA BEL
    1955 /1/ +GFR

220 FRA 1816–1942 /1/ BAD ITA NTH GER SPA SWZ /2/ PAP SIC
  TUS UK /3/ UK POR NTH DEN SWD SPA
    1826 /3/ +BRA
    1830 /1/ +BEL −NTH /3/ +SPA +TUR
    1842 /2/ +MOD
    1847 /3/ +MOR
    1860 /2/ −MOD −PAP −TUS /3/ +CHN
    1861 /2/ −SIC
    1870 /1/ −BAD
    1878 /3/ −SWD
    1884 /3/ +GER
    1885 /3/ +BEL
    1887 /3/ +THI
    1890 /3/ +ITA
    1898 /3/ +ETH
    1911 /3/ −MOR
    1912 /3/ −TUR
    1916 /3/ −GER
    1917 /3/ −DEN
    1919 /3/ +TUR
    1920 /1/ +LUX /3/ +CAN +LIB
    1926 /3/ +YAR
    1932 /3/ +IRQ
    1936 /3/ −ETH
    1940 /1/ −LUX
    1941 /3/ +ETH
220 FRA 1945–1965 /1/ BEL ITA LUX SPA SWZ /2/ UK /3/ BRA CHN EGY
  ETH IRQ LBR POR THI TUR USA
    1947 /3/ +IND −IRQ −TUR
    1948 /3/ +BUR
    1952 /3/ +LIB
    1953 /3/ +KHM
    1955 /1/ +GFR /3/ −BUR −CHN −IND −KHM −THI
    1956 /3/ +MOR +SUD +TUN −USA
    1957 /3/ −EGY +GHA
    1958 /3/ +GUI
    1960 /3/ +MAA +MLI +NIR +SOM
    1961 /3/ −GHA −GUI −LBR −POR −SUD
    1962 /3/ −MOR
    1963 /3/ −LIB −MAA −MLI −MOR −NIR −TUN

225 SWZ 1816–1965 /1/ FRA ITA AUS BAD WRT BAV
    1870 /1/ +GER −BAV −WRT −BAD

```
1918 /1/ −AUS
1919 /1/ +AUS
1938 /1/ −AUS
1942 /1/ −FRA
1944 /1/ +FRA
1955 /1/ +AUS +GFR
```

230 SPA 1816–1965 /1/ POR FRA /3/ NTH FRA UK USA DEN POR CHN
    SWD
```
1823 /3/ +USR
1831 /3/ −USR +MEX
1847 /2/ +MOR /3/ +MOR
1859 /3/ +HAI
1862 /2/ +DEN
1878 /3/ −SWD
1884 /3/ +GER
1887 /3/ +DOM
1895 /3/ +JPN
1898 /3/ −NTH −DEN −UK −USA −HAI −DOM −MEX
1911 /2/ −MOR /3/ −MOR
1916 /3/ −GER
1942 /1/ −FRA /3/ −FRA
1944 /1/ +FRA /3/ +FRA
1956 /2/ +MOR /3/ +MOR
1960 /3/ +CAO +GAB +MAA
1962 /2/ +ALG
```

235 POR 1816–1965 /1/ SPA /3/ SPA FRA UK NTH CHN
```
1847 /2/ +MOR
1885 /3/ +GER +BEL
1911 /2/ −MOR
1919 /3/ −GER
1920 /3/ +SAF
1940 /3/ −BEL −NTH
1942 /3/ −FRA +JPN
1945 /3/ −JPN +NTH +BEL
1947 /3/ +IND
1949 /3/ +INS
1956 /2/ +MOR
1958 /3/ +GUI
1960 /3/ +CON +SEN +ZAI
1961 /3/ −BEL −FRA +TAZ
1962 /3/ −IND
1964 /3/ +MAW +ZAM
1965 /3/ +RHO
```

240 HAN 1838–1866 /1/ NTH GER DEN /2/ UK
    1843 /1/ +MEC

245 BAV 1816–1870 /1/ AUH SWZ WRT SAX HSE BAD HSG
    1866 /1/ +GER −HSE
    1867 /1/ −HSG −SAX

255 GER 1816–1945 /1/ AUH BAV FRA HSE HSG NTH SAX USR /2/ SWD
DEN
    1830 /1/ +BEL
    1838 /1/ +HAN
    1843 /1/ +MEC
    1866 /1/ −HAN −HSE −SAX +DEN +BAV /3/ +UK
    1867 /1/ −HSG −MEC −SAX +BAD
    1870 /1/ −BAV
    1871 /1/ +SWZ /2/ +DEN
    1884 /3/ +FRA +SPA
    1885 /3/ +BEL +NTH +POR
    1898 /3/ +CHN
    1899 /3/ +USA
    1914 /3/ −CHN −NTH
    1916 /3/ −FRA −SPA
    1918 /1/ +CZE +LIT /3/ −BEL −POR −UK
    1919 /1/ +POL −AUH +AUS /3/ −USA
    1920 /1/ +LUX
    1938 /1/ −AUS
    1939 /1/ −CZE −POL
    1940 /1/ −BEL −DEN −LIT −LUX −NTH /2/ −DEN
    1942 /1/ −FRA
    1944 /1/ +FRA +LUX
    1945 /1/ +BEL +CZE +DEN +NTH +POL /2/ +DEN

260 GFR 1955–1965 /1/ AUS BEL CZE DEN FRA GDR LUX NTH SWZ

265 GDR 1954–1965 /1/ CZE POL /2/ DEN SWD /3/ FRA UK USA
    1955 /1/ +GFR
    1956 /3/ −FRA −UK −USA

267 BAD 1816–1870 /1/ FRA BAV SWZ WRT HSG AUH
    1867 /1/ +GER −HSG

269 SAX 1816–1867 /1/ GER AUH BAV

271 WRT 1816–1870 /1/ BAV BAD AUH SWZ

273 HSE 1816–1866 /1/ HAN GER HSG BAV

275 HSG 1816–1867 /1/ HSE GER BAV BAD
    1866 /1/ −HSE

280 MEC 1843–1867 /1/ GER HAN /2/ DEN SWD
    1866 /1/ −HAN

290 POL 1919–1939 /1/ LAT LIT USR RUM CZE GER /2/ SWD DEN
    1939 /1/ −CZE −LAT −LIT
290 POL 1945–1965 /1/ CZE USR /2/ DEN SWE
    1954 /1/ +GDR

300 AUH 1816–1918 /1/ BAD BAV ITA GER PAP SAX TUR USR WRT SWZ
    /2/ SIC
    1851 /1/ +PMA
    1860 /1/ −PAP −PMA
    1861 /2/ −SIC
    1867 /1/ −SAX
    1870 /1/ −BAV −BAD
    1878 /1/ +RUM +YUG −TUR

305 AUS 1919–1938 /1/ CZE HUN YUG ITA SWZ GER
305 AUS 1955–1965 /1/ CZE GFR HUN ITA SWZ YUG

310 HUN 1919–1945 /1/ RUM CZE YUG AUS
    1938 /1/ −AUS
    1939 /1/ −CZE +GER
    1941 /1/ −YUG
    1944 /1/ +YUG
    1945 /1/ −GER +CZE
    1955 /1/ +AUS

315 CZE 1918–1939 /1/ RUM GER
    1919 /1/ +POL +AUS +HUN
    1938 /1/ −AUS
315 CZE 1945–1965 /1/ HUN POL USR /3/ USA
    1954 /1/ +GDR
    1955 /1/ +AUS +GFR
    1956 /3/ −USA
325 ITA 1816–1860 /1/ FRA AUH SWZ TUS /2/ PAP SIC
    1842 /1/ +MOD
    1851 /1/ +PMA
    1860 /1/ +SIC /2/ −PAP
    1861 /1/ −SIC /2/ −SIC

325 ITA 1861–1943 /1/ AUH FRA SWZ /2/ GRE SPA TUR /3/ UK
    1862 /3/ −UK

```
1889 /3/ +FRA
1890 /3/ +UK +TUR
1898 /3/ +ETH
1912 /2/ -TUR
1914 /2/ +ALB
1919 /1/ -AUH +AUS +YUG
1926 /3/ +YAR
1927 /3/ +SAU
1936 /3/ -ETH
1937 /3/ +EGY
1938 /1/ -AUS
1939 /2/ -ALB
1940 /3/ -SAU
1941 /1/ -YUG /2/ -GRE /3/ +ETH
1942 /1/ -FRA /3/ -UK -EGY -ETH -FRA -YAR
1944 /1/ +YUG /2/ +ALB /3/ +UK +FRA
1945 /2/ +GRE /3/ +EGY +USA
1947 /3/ -EGY
1950 /3/ +ETH
1955 /1/ +AUS
1956 /2/ +TUN /3/ -USA
1961 /3/ -ETH -UK
1962 /2/ +ALG
1964 /2/ +MLT
```

327 PAP 1816–1860 /1/ AUH TUS SIC /2/ FRA ITA
```
    1842 /1/ +MOD
```

329 SIC 1816–1861 /1/ PAP /2/ AUH TUR ITA /3/ FRA UK
```
    1828 /2/ +GRE
    1860 /1/ +ITA -PAP
```

332 MOD 1842–1860 /1/ TUS PAP AUH ITA /2/ FRN
```
    1851 /1/ +PMA
```

335 PMA 1851–1860 /1/ ITA MOD AUH

337 TUS 1816–1860 /1/ PAP ITA /2/ FRA
```
    1842 /1/ +MOD
```

338 MLT 1964–1965 /2/ ITA LIB TUN

339 ALB 1914–1939 /1/ YUG GRE /2/ ITA
339 ALB 1944–1965 /1/ YUG /2/ ITA
```
    1945 /1/ +GRE
```

345 YUG 1878–1941 /1/ TUR AUH RUM
    1908 /1/ +BUL
    1913 /1/ −TUR +GRE
    1914 /1/ +ALB
    1918 /1/ −AUH
    1919 /1/ +AUS +HUN +ITA
    1938 /1/ −AUS
    1939 /1/ −ALB
    1941 /1/ −GRE
345 YUG 1944–1965 /1/ ALB BUL HUN ITA RUM
    1945 /1/ +GRE; /3/ +UK +USR
    1955 /1/ +AUS
    1956 /3/ −UK −USR

350 GRE 1828–1941 /1/ TUR /2/ SIC /3/ UK
    1861 /2/ −SIC +ITA
    1864 /3/ −UK
    1878 /3/ +UK
    1908 /1/ +BUL
    1913 /1/ +GRE
    1914 /1/ +ALB
    1939 /1/ −ALB
350 GRE 1945–1965 /1/ ALB BUL TUR YUG /2/ ITA
    1952 /2/ +LIB

352 CYP 1960–1965 /2/ ISR LEB SYR TUR

355 BUL 1908–1945 /1/ RUM YUG TUR
    1913 /1/ +GRE
    1941 /1/ −YUG −GRE
    1944 /1/ +YUG
    1945 /1/ +GRE /2/ USR

360 RUM 1878–1965 /1/ YUG USR AUH TUR
    1908 /1/ +BUL −TUR
    1918 /1/ +CZE −AUH +HUN
    1939 /1/ −CZE
    1941 /1/ −YUG
    1945 /1/ +CZE

365 USR 1816–1945 /1/ AUH GER SWD TUR /3/ UK
    1831 /3/ +MEX
    1848 /3/ −MEX
    1855 /1/ +IRA
    1860 /1/ +CHN /2/ +JPN
    1867 /3/ −UK +USA

1878 /1/ +RUM
1888 /1/ +KOR
1905 /1/ +NOR −KOR /3/ +JPN
1910 /1/ +JPN
1918 /1/ +EST +LAT −GER
1919 /1/ −AUH +FIN +POL −SWD
1920 /1/ +AFG
1921 /1/ +MON
1939 /1/ −POL +GER
1940 /1/ −EST −LAT
1945 /1/ +CZE −GER +HUN −JPN +POL /2/ +BUL −JPN +SWD
  /3/ − JPN +USA +YUG
1948 /1/ +PRK
1952 /2/ +JPN
1956 /3/ −UK −USA −YUG
1959 /3/ −USA /2/ +USA

366 EST 1918–1940 /1/ USR LAT /2/ SWD
1919 /1/ +FIN

367 LAT 1918–1940 /1/ LIT EST USR /2/ SWD
1919 /2/ +FIN +POL
1939 /1/ −POL

368 LIT 1918–1940 /1/ LAT GER /2/ SWD
1919 /1/ +POL
1939 /1/ −POL

375 FIN 1919–1965 /1/ USR NOR SWD /2/ EST LAT
1940 /1/ −NOR /2/ −EST −LAT
1945 /1/ +NOR

380 SWD 1816–1945 /1/ USR /2/ DEN GER /3/ DEN UK FRA SPA
1843 /2/ +MEC
1867 /2/ −MEC
1878 /3/ −DEN −UK −FRA −SPA
1905 /1/ +NOR
1918 /2/ +EST +LIT +LAT
1919 /1/ +FIN −USR /2/ +POL
1939 /2/ −POL
1940 /1/ −NOR /2/ −EST −LAT −LIT −DEN
1944 /2/ +USR
1945 /1/ +NOR /2/ +POL +DEN −GER
1954 /2/ +GDR

385 NOR 1905–1940 /1/ SWD USR /2/ DEN
    1919 /1/ +FIN
385 NOR 1945–1965 /1/ SWD USR FIN /2/ DEN

390 DEN 1816–1940 /1/ GER /2/ GER SWD /3/ UK FRA SPA NTH SWD
    1838 /1/ +HAN
    1843 /1/ +MEC
    1850 /3/ −NTH
    1862 /3/ −SPA −FRA
    1866 /1/ −HAN +GER
    1867 /1/ −MEC
    1878 /3/ −SWD
    1890 /3/ −UK
    1898 /3/ +USA
    1905 /2/ +NOR
    1917 /3/ −USA
    1919 /2/ +POL
    1920 /3/ +CAN
    1939 /2/ −POL

390 DEN 1945–1965 /2/ NOR NTH POL SWD /3/ UK CAN
    1953 /2/ +CAN /3/ −CAN
    1954 /2/ +GDR
    1955 /1/ +GFR
    1956 /3/ −UK

395 ICE 1944–1965

420 GAM 1965 /1/ SEN

432 MLI 1960–1965 /1/ GUI IVO MAA NIR SEN UPP /3/ FRA
    1962 /1/ +ALG
    1963 /3/ −FRA

433 SEN 1960–1965 /1/ GUI MAA MLI /3/ POR UK
    1965 /1/ +GAM

434 BEN 1960–1965 /1/ NIG NIR TOG UPP

435 MAA 1960–1965 /1/ MLI SEN /3/ FRA SPA
    1962 /1/ +ALG
    1963 /3/ −FRA

436 NIR 1960–1965 /1/ BEN CHA LIB MLI NIG UPP /2/ CAO /3/ FRA
    1962 /1/ +ALG
    1963 /3/ −FRA

437 IVO 1960–1965 /1/ GHA GUI LBR MLI UPP

438 GUI 1958–1965 /1/ LBR /3/ FRA POR UK
    1960 /1/ +IVO +MLI +SEN
    1961 /1/ +SIE /3/ −FRA
    1962 /3/ −UK

439 UPP 1960–1965 /1/ BEN GHA IVO MLI NIR TOG

450 LBR 1945–1965 /3/ FRA UK
    1958 /1/ +GUI
    1960 /1/ +IVO
    1961 /1/ +SIE /3/ −FRA
    1962 /3/ −UK

451 SIE 1961–1965 /1/ GUI LBR

452 GHA 1957–1965 /3/ FRA UK
    1960 /1/ +IVO +TOG +UPP
    1961 /3/ −FRA −UK

461 TOG 1960–1965 /1/ BEN GHA UPP

471 CAO 1960–1965 /1/ CEN CHA CON GAB NIG /2/ NIR /3/ SPA

475 NIG 1960–1965 /1/ BEN CAO NIR /2/ CHA

481 GAB 1960–1965 /1/ CAO CON /3/ SPA

482 CEN 1960–1965 /1/ CAO CHA CON SUD ZAI

483 CHA 1960–1965 /1/ CAO CEN LIB NIR SUD /2/ NIG

484 CON 1960–1965 /1/ CAO CEN GAB ZAI /3/ POR UK
    1965 /3/ −UK

490 ZAI 1960–1965 /1/ CEN CON SUD /3/ POR UK
    1961 /1/ +TAZ
    1962 /1/ +BUI +RWA +UGA
    1964 /1/ +ZAM
    1965 /3/ −UK

500 UGA 1962–1965 /1/ RWA SUD TAZ ZAI /3/ UK
    1963 /1/ +KEN
    1964 /3/ −UK

501 KEN 1963–1965 /1/ ETH SOM SUD TAZ UGA /2/ ZAN

510 TAZ 1961–1965 /1/ ZAI /3/ POR UK
    1962 /1/ +BUI +RWA +UGA
    1963 /1/ +KEN /2/ +ZAN
    1964 /1/ +MAW +ZAM
    1965 /3/ −UK

511 ZAN 1963–1965 /2/ KEN TAZ

516 BUI 1962–1965 /1/ RWA TAZ ZAI

517 RWA 1962–1965 /1/ BUI TAZ UGA ZAI

520 SOM 1960–1965 /1/ ETH /2/ YAR /3/ FRA UK
    1963 /1/ +KEN
    1964 /3/ −UK

530 ETH 1898–1936 /3/ FRA UK ITA
530 ETH 1941–1965 /2/ SAU YAR /3/ ITA FRA UK
    1942 /3/ −FRA −ITA
    1944 /3/ +FRA
    1945 /3/ +EGY
    1950 /3/ +ITA
    1956 /1/ +SUD /3/ −UK −EGY
    1960 /1/ +SOM
    1961 /3/ −ITA
    1963 /1/ +KEN
    1964 /3/ −UK

551 ZAM 1964–1965 /1/ MAW TAZ ZAI /3/ POR SAF UK
    1965 /1/ +RHO

552 RHO 1965 /1/ SAF ZAM /3/ POR UK

553 MAW 1964–1965 /1/ TAZ ZAM /3/ POR

560 SAF 1920–1965 /3/ POR UK
    1964 /3/ +ZAM
    1965 /1/ +RHO

600 MOR 1847–1911 /2/ SPA POR /3/ SPA FRA UK

600 MOR 1956–1965 /2/ POR SPA /3/ FRA SPA UK
    1962 /1/ +ALG /3/ −FRA

615 ALG 1962–1965 /1/ LIB MAA MLI MOR NIR TUN /2/ ITA SPA

616 TUN 1956–1965 /1/ LIB /2/ ITA /3/ FRA
    1962 /1/ +ALG
    1963 /3/ −FRA
    1964 /2/ +MLT

620 LIB 1920–1965 /3/ FRA UK
    1942 /3/ −FRA
    1944 /3/ +FRA
    1956 /1/ +SUD +TUN
    1957 /3/ −UK
    1960 /1/ +CHA +NIR
    1962 /1/ +ALG
    1963 /3/ −FRA
    1964 /2/ +MLT

625 SUD 1956–1965 /1/ EGY ETH LIB /2/ SAU /3/ BEL FRA UK
    1960 /1/ +CEN +CHA +ZAI
    1961 /3/ −BEL −FRA
    1962 /1/ +UGA
    1963 /1/ +KEN
    1964 /3/ −UK

630 IRA 1855–1965 /1/ TUR USR /3/ UK
    1920 /1/ +AFG
    1927 /2/ +SAU
    1932 /1/ +IRQ
    1947 /1/ +PAK
    1948 /3/ −UK
    1961 /2/ +KUW

640 TUR 1816–1965 /1/ USR AUH /2/ SIC /3/ UK
    1828 /1/ +GRE
    1830 /3/ +FRA
    1855 /1/ +IRA
    1860 /2/ +ITA −SIC
    1864 /3/ −UK
    1878 /1/ +RUM +YUG −AUH /2/ −ITA /3/ +UK
    1890 /3/ +ITA
    1908 /1/ +BUL −RUM −YUG
    1912 /3/ +ITA −FRA
    1920 /3/ +FRA
    1932 /1/ +IRQ
    1941 /1/ −GRE

    1942 /3/ −FRA
    1944 /3/ +FRA
    1945 /1/ +GRE /2/ +RUM
    1946 /1/ +SYR /2/ +LEB
    1947 /3/ −FRA
    1960 /2/ +CYP

645 IRQ 1932–1965 /1/ IRA SAU TUR /3/ FRA UK
    1946 /1/ +JOR +SYR
    1947 /3/ −FRA
    1961 /1/ +KUW
    1962 /3/ −UK

651 EGY 1855–1882 /3/ UK
651 EGY 1937–1965 /2/ SAU /3/ ITA UK
    1943 /3/ −ITA
    1945 /3/ BEL ETH FRA
    1946 /2/ +JOR +LEB
    1947 /3/ −ITA
    1948 /1/ +ISR
    1952 /1/ +LIB
    1956 /1/ +SUD /3/ −ETH
    1957 /3/ −BEL −UK −FRA

652 SYR 1946–1965 /1/ IRQ JOR LEB TUR /3/ UK
    1948 /1/ +ISR
    1949 /3/ −UK
    1960 /2/ +CYP

660 LEB 1946–1965 /1/ SYR /2/ EGY TUR /3/ UK
    1948 /1/ +ISR
    1949 /3/ −UK
    1960 /2/ +CYP

663 JOR 1946–1965 /1/ IRQ SAU SYR /2/ EGY /3/ UK
    1948 /1/ +ISR
    1949 /3/ −UK

666 ISR 1948–1965 /1/ EGY JOR LEB SYR /2/ SAU
    1960 /2/ +CYP

670 SAU 1927–1965 /1/ YAR /2/ IRA /3/ ITA UK
    1932 /1/ +IRQ
    1937 /2/ +EGY
    1941 /3/ −ITA
    1946 /1/ +JOR

```
    1948 /2/ +ISR
    1956 /2/ +SUD
    1961 /1/ +KUW

678 YAR 1926–1965 /3/ UK FRA ITA
    1927 /1/ +SAU
    1941 /3/ −ITA; /2/ +ETH
    1960 /2/ +SOM
    1963 /3/ −UK

690 KUW 1961–1965 /1/ IRQ SAU /2/ IRA

700 AFG 1920–1965 /1/ IRA USR CHN /3/ UK
    1947 /1/ +IND +PAK
    1948 /3/ −UK

710 CHN 1860–1965 /1/ USR /3/ FRA UK SPA POR
    1888 /1/ +KOR
    1895 /3/ −SPA +JPN
    1898 /3/ +GER
    1905 /1/ −KOR
    1914 /3/ −GER
    1920 /1/ +NEP +AFG
    1921 /1/ +MON
    1943 /3/ −FRA
    1944 /3/ +FRA
    1947 /1/ +IND +PAK
    1948 /1/ +BUR +PRK
    1949 /2/ +ROK +TAW
    1952 /2/ +JPN
    1954 /1/ +DRV +LAO /2/ +RVN
    1955 /3/ −FRA

712 MON 1921–1965 /1/ USR CHN

713 TAW 1949–1965 /2/ CHN PHI
    1952 /2/ +JPN

730 KOR 1888–1905 /1/ CHN USR /2/ JPN

731 PRK 1948–1965 /1/ CHN USR /3/ USA
    1949 /1/ +ROK /3/ −USA

732 ROK 1949–1965 /1/ PRK /2/ CHN
    1952 /2/ +JPN
```

740 JPN 1860–1945 /2/ USR
    1888 /2/ +KOR
    1895 /3/ +SPN
    1898 /3/ − SPN +CHN +FRA +GER +UK +USA
    1905 /3/ +USR −KOR
    1910 /1/ +USR
    1930 /3/ −UK
    1942 /3/ +POR
    1945 /3/ −CHN −POR −USA −USR
740 JPN 1952–1965 /2/ CHN ROK TAW USR

750 IND 1947–1965 /1/ AFG CHN NEP PAK /3/ FRA POR
    1948 /1/ +BUR /2/ +SRI /3/ +UK
    1949 /3/ −UK
    1955 /3/ −FRA
    1962 /3/ −POR

770 PAK 1947–1965 /1/ AFG CHN IND IRA
    1948 /1/ +BUR /3/ +UK
    1949 /3/ −UK

775 BUR 1948–1965 /1/ CHN IND PAK THI /3/ FRA
    1954 /1/ +LAO
    1955 /3/ −FRA

780 SRI 1948–1965 /2/ IND

781 MAD 1957–1965 /1/ THI

790 NEP 1920–1965 /3/ UK
    1945 /1/ +CHN
    1947 /1/ +IND
    1948 /3/ −UK

800 THI 1887–1965 /3/ FRA UK
    1942 /3/ −FRA
    1944 /3/ +FRA
    1948 /1/ +BUR
    1949 /2/ +INS
    1953 /1/ +KHM
    1954 /1/ +LAO
    1955 /3/ −FRA
    1957 /1/ +MAD +MAL
    1958 /3/ −UK

811 KHM 1953–1965 /1/ THI /3/ FRA
    1954 /1/ +LAO +RVN
    1955 /3/ −FRA

812 LAO 1954–1965 /1/ BUR CHN DRV KHM RVN THI

816 DRV 1954–1965 /1/ CHN LAO RVN

817 RVN 1954–1965 /1/ DRV KHM LAO /2/ CHN

820 MAL 1957–1965 /1/ THI /2/ INS
    1963 /1/ +INS /2/ +PHI −INS /3/ +UK
    1965 /1/ +SIN

830 SIN 1965 /1/ MAL /2/ INS

840 PHI 1949–1965 /2/ INS TAW
    1963 /2/ +MAL

850 INS 1949–1965 /2/ AUL PHI THI /3/ POR UK
    1957 /2/ +MAL
    1963 /1/ +MAL /2/ −MAL
    1964 /3/ −UK
    1965 /2/ +SIN

900 AUL 1920–1965 /3/ NTH JPN
    1940 /3/ −NTH
    1945 /3/ +NTH −JPN
    1949 /2/ +INS
    1964 /3/ −NTH

920 NEW 1920–1965

Abbreviations

AFG	Afghanistan		BAH	Bahrein
ALB	Albania		BAV	Bavaria
ALG	Algeria		BEL	Belgium
ARG	Argentina		BEN	Benin/Dahomey
AUH	Austria-Hungary		BHM	Bahamas
AUL	Australia		BHU	Bhutan
AUS	Austria		BNG	Bangladesh
BAD	Baden		BOL	Bolivia

BRA	Brazil	IND	India
BUI	Burundi	INS	Indonesia
BUL	Bulgaria	IRE	Ireland
BUR	Burma	IRA	Iran (Persia)
CAN	Canada	IRQ	Iraq
CAO	Cameroun	ISR	Israel
CEN	Central African Republic	ITA	Italy/Sardinia
CHA	Chad	IVO	Ivory Coast
CHL	Chile	JAM	Jamaica
CHN	China	JOR	Jordan
COL	Colombia	JPN	Japan
CON	Congo	KEN	Kenya
COS	Costa Rica	KHM	Kampuchea (Cambodia)
CUB	Cuba	KOR	Korea
CYP	Cyprus	KUW	Kuwait
CZE	Czechoslovakia	LAO	Laos
DEN	Denmark	LAT	Latvia
DOM	Dominican Republic	LBR	Liberia
DRV	Vietnam, Democratic	LEB	Lebanon
	Republic	LIB	Libya
ECU	Ecuador	LIT	Lithuania
EGY	Egypt/UAR	LUX	Luxemburg
EST	Estonia	MAA	Mauritania
ETH	Ethiopia	MAD	Maldive Islands
FIN	Finland	MAG	Malagasy
FRA	France	MAL	Malaysia
GAB	Gabon	MAW	Malawi
GDR	German Democratic	MEC	Mecklenburg Schwerin
	Republic	MEX	Mexico
GFR	German Federal Republic	MLI	Mali
GHA	Ghana	MLT	Malta
GMY	Germany/Prussia	MOD	Modena
GRC	Greece	MON	Mongolia
GUA	Guatemala	MOR	Morocco
GUI	Guinea	NEP	Nepal
HAI	Haiti	NEW	New Zealand
HAN	Hanover	NIC	Nicaragua
HON	Honduras	NIG	Nigeria
HSE	Hesse Electoral	NIR	Niger
HSG	Hesse Grand Ducal	NOR	Norway
HUN	Hungary	NTH	Netherlands
ICE	Iceland	OMA	Oman

PAK	Pakistan		SUD	Sudan
PAN	Panama		SWD	Sweden
PAP	Papal States		SWZ	Switzerland
PAR	Paraguay		SYR	Syria
PER	Peru		TAW	Taiwan
PHI	Philippines		TAZ	Tanzania/Tanganyika
PMA	Parma		THI	Thailand
POL	Poland		TOG	Togo
POR	Portugal		TRI	Trinidad
PRK	Korea, Democratic People's Republic		TUN	Tunisia
			TUR	Turkey/Ottoman Empire
QAT	Qatar		TUS	Tuscany
RHO	Rhodesia		UAE	United Arab Emirates
ROK	Korea, Republic of		UGA	Uganda
RUM	Rumania		UK	United Kingdom
RWA	Rwanda		UPP	Upper Volta
SAF	South Africa		URU	Uruguay
SAL	El Salvador		USA	United States of America
SAU	Saudi Arabia		USR	USSR (Russia)
SAX	Saxony		VEN	Venezuela
SEN	Senegal		WRT	Wuerttemburg
SIC	Two Sicilies		YAR	Yemen Arab Republic
SIE	Sierra Leone		YUG	Yugoslavia/Serbia
SIN	Singapore		ZAI	Zaire (Congo, Kinshasa)
SOM	Somalia		ZAM	Zambia
SPN	Spain		ZAN	Zanzibar
SRI	Sri Lanka (Ceylon)			

Bibliography

Alcock, Norman Z. 1972. *The War Disease*. Oakville, Ont.: Canadian Peace Research Institute Press.

Altfeld, Michael, and Bruce Bueno de Mesquita. 1979. "Choosing Sides in Wars." *International Studies Quarterly* 23: 87–112.

Anselin, L., and J. O'Loughlin. 1989. "Spatial Econometric Analysis of International Conflict." In *Dynamics and Conflict in Regional Structural Change,* ed. M. Chatterji and R. Kuenne. London: Macmillan.

Beer, Francis A. 1981. *Peace against War*. San Francisco: W. H. Freeman.

Berridge, G. R. 1989. "Ententes and Alliances." *Review of International Studies* 15:251–60.

Berry, B. J. L. 1969. "A Synthesis of Formal and Functional Regions Using a General Field Theory of Spatial Behavior." In *Spatial Analysis,* ed. B. J. L. Berry and D. F. Marble. Englewood Cliffs, NJ: Prentice Hall.

Boulding, Kenneth. 1962. *Conflict and Defense*. New York: Harper & Row.

Bueno de Mesquita, Bruce. 1981. *The War Trap*. New Haven: Yale University Press.

Bueno de Mesquita, Bruce. 1984. "A Critique of 'A Critique of *The War Trap*.'" *Journal of Conflict Resolution* 28:341–60.

Bueno de Mesquita, Bruce, and David Lalman. 1986. "Reason and War." *American Political Science Review* 80:1113–29.

Choucri, N., and R. C. North. 1975. *Nations in Conflict*. San Francisco: W. H. Freeman.

Cliff, A. D., and J. K. Ord. 1981. *Spatial Processes: Models and Applications*. London: Pion.

Cohen, S. B. 1963. *Geography and Politics in A World Divided*. New York: Random House.

Coleman, James S. 1964. *Introduction to Mathematical Sociology*. New York: Free Press.

Converse, Elizabeth. 1968. "The War of All against All: A Review of the *Journal of Conflict Resolution, 1957–1968*." *Journal of Conflict Resolution* 12:471–532.

Davis, William, George Duncan, and Randolph Siverson. 1978. "The Dynamics of Warfare, 1816–1965." *American Journal of Political Science* 22:772–92.

Deutsch, Karl W. 1967. "Changing Images of International Conflict." *Journal of Social Issues*. 23:91–107.

Diehl, P. F. 1985. "Contiguity and Military Escalation in Major Power Rivalries, 1816–1980." *Journal of Politics* 47:1203–11.

Diehl, P. F. 1987. "Getting Back to the Basics: Territory as a Source of Conflict."

Presented at the annual meeting of the American Political Science Association, Chicago.

Diehl, Paul. 1988. "Geography and War: A Review and Assessment of the Empirical Literature." Presented at the annual meeting of the International Studies Association, St. Louis.

Diehl, Paul F., and Gary Goertz. 1988. "Territorial Changes and Militarized Conflict." *Journal of Conflict Resolution* 32:103–22.

Engel, Josef, ed. 1962. *Grosser Historischer Weltatlas.* Munich: Bayerischer Schulbuck-Verlag.

Faber, Jan, Henk Houweling, and Jan Siccama. 1984. "Diffusion of War: Some Theoretical Considerations and Empirical Evidence." *Journal of Peace Research* 21:277–88.

Fox, W. T. R. 1985. "Geopolitics and International Relations." In *On Geopolitics: Classical and Nuclear,* ed. C. E. Zoppo and C. Zorgbibe. Boston: Martinus Nijhoff.

Galtung, Johan. 1969. "Violence, Peace and Peace Research." *Journal of Peace Research* 6:167–91.

Galtung, Johan. 1985. "Twenty-five Years of Peace Research: Ten Challenges and Some Responses." *Journal of Peace Research* 22:141–58.

Gamson, W. A. 1961. "A Theory of Coalition Formation." *American Sociological Review* 26:373–82.

Garnham, David. 1988. "Balancing or Bandwagoning: Empirical Evidence from 19th and 20th Century Europe." Presented at the International Studies Association, St. Louis.

Garthoff, Raymond L. 1989. *Reflections on the Cuban Missile Crisis.* Washington, DC: Brookings.

Giddens, A. 1984. *The Constitution of Society.* Berkeley: University of California Press.

Gilpin, Robert. 1981. *War and Change in World Politics.* New York: Cambridge University Press.

Gleditsch, Nils P. 1969. "The International Airline Network: A Test of the Zipf and Stouffer Hypotheses." *Peace Research Society: Papers.* 11:123–53.

Gochman, Charles S., and Alan Ned Sabrosky, eds. 1990a. *Prisoners of War? Nation-States in the Modern Era.* Lexington, MA: D. C. Heath.

Gochman, Charles S., and Alan Ned Sabrosky. 1990b. "Prisoners of War? A Preview." In *Prisoners of War?* ed. Charles S. Gochman and A. N. Sabrosky. Lexington, MA: D. C. Heath.

Goertz, G. 1989. "Contextual Theories and Indicators in World Politics." Center for International Economic History, University of Geneva.

Goldstein, Joshua. 1988. *Long Cycles.* New Haven: Yale University Press.

Gould, Peter. 1969. *Spatial Diffusion.* Washington: Association of American Geographers, Resource Paper No. 4.

Gray, Colin. 1977. *The Geopolitics of the Nuclear Era.* New York: Crane Russak.

Hagerstrand, T. 1967. *Innovation as a Spatial Process.* Chicago: University of Chicago Press.

Hammond Historical Atlas of the World. 1984. Maplewood, NJ: Hammond.

Henige, David P. 1970. *Colonial Governors from the 15th Century to the Present.* Madison: University of Wisconsin Press.

Holsti, O. R., P. T. Hopmann, and J. S. Sullivan. 1973. *Unity and Disintegration in International Alliances.* New York: Wiley.

Holsti, Ole R., and Robert C. North. 1965. "The History of Human Conflict." In *The Nature of Human Conflict,* ed. Elton McNeil. Englewood Cliffs, NJ: Prentice Hall.

Horvath, William J., and Caxton C. Foster. 1963. "Stochastic Models of War Alliances." *Journal of Conflict Resolution* 7:110–16.

Houweling, Henk W., and Jan G. Siccama. 1985. "The Epidemiology of War, 1816–1980." *Journal of Conflict Resolution* 29:641–63.

Huth, Paul, and Bruce Russett. 1984. "What Makes Deterrence Work? Cases From 1900 to 1980." *World Politics* 36:496–526.

Huth, Paul, and Bruce Russett. 1988. "Deterrence Failure and Crisis Escalation." *International Studies Quarterly* 32:29–46.

International Studies Quarterly. 1983. "An Exchange on the Interstate System and the Capitalist World Economy." 27:341–74.

Job, Brian L. 1976. "Membership in International Alliances, 1815–1965." In *Mathematical Models in International Relations,* ed. Dina A. Zinnes and John Gillespie. New York: Praeger.

Job, Brian L. 1981. "Grins without Cats: In Pursuit of Knowledge of International Alliances." In *Cumulation in International Relations Research,* ed. P. T. Hopmann et al. Denver: University of Denver Monograph Series in World Affairs.

Kann, R. A. 1976. "Alliances Versus Ententes." *World Politics* 28:611–21.

Kegley, Charles W., Jr., and Gregory Raymond. 1990. "The End of Alliances?" *USA Today* 118, no. 254: 32–34.

Kende, Istvan. 1971. "Twenty-five Years of Local Wars." *Journal of Peace Research* 8:5–27.

Kende, Istvan. 1978. "Wars of Ten Years (1967–1976)." *Journal of Peace Research* 15:227–41.

Kennedy, Paul. 1987. *The Rise and Fall of the Great Powers.* New York: Random House.

Kirby, A. 1986. "Review Essay: Where's the Theory?" *Political Geography Quarterly* 5:187–92.

Kirby, A. 1988. "Context, Common Sense and the Reality of Place: A Critical Reading of Meyrowitz." *Journal for the Theory of Social Behavior* 18:239–50.

Kirby, A., and M.D. Ward, 1987. "Space, Spatiality, Geography, Territoriality, Context, Locale—and Conflict." Presented at the annual meeting of the American Political Science Association, Chicago.

Klingman, David. 1979. "Theory and Method in the Study of Diffusion." Presented at the annual meeting of the Midwest Political Science Association, Chicago.

Kratochwil, F. 1986. "Of Systems, Boundaries and Territoriality. *World Politics* 39:27–52.

Leng, Russell J., and Charles S. Gochman. 1982. "Dangerous Disputes: A Study of Conflict Behavior and War." *American Journal of Political Science* 26 (November): 664–87.

Levy, Jack S. 1981. "Alliance Formation and War Behavior." *Journal of Conflict Resolution* 25:581–613.

Levy, Jack S. 1983. *War in the Modern Great Power System 1495–1975.* Lexington: The University Press of Kentucky.

Levy, Jack S. 1989. "The Causes of War: A Review of Theories and Evidence." In Vol. 1 of *Behavior, Society, and Nuclear War,* ed. Phillip E. Tetlock. New York: Oxford University Press.

Lewis-Beck, Michael. 1980. *Applied Regression Analysis.* Sage University Paper Series on Quantitative Applications in the Social Sciences, 07–22. Beverly Hills and London: Sage.

Li, Richard, and William Thompson. 1975. "The 'Coup Contagion' Hypothesis." *Journal of Conflict Resolution* 19:63–88.

Mackinder, Halford J. 1919. *Democratic Ideals and Reality.* New York: Henry Holt.

Mahan, Alfred Thayer. 1890. *The Influence of Sea Power upon History.* Annapolis, MD: Naval Institute Press.

Maoz, Zeev. 1982. *Paths to Conflict.* Boulder, CO: Westview.

Midlarksy, Manus. 1970. "Mathematical Models of Instability and a Theory of Diffusion." *International Studies Quarterly* 14:60–84.

Midlarsky, Manus. 1975. *On War.* New York: Free Press.

Midlarsky, Manus, ed. 1989. *Handbook of War Studies.* Boston: Unwin Hyman.

Modelski, George. 1987. *Long Cycles in World Politics.* Seattle: University of Washington Press.

Modelski, George, and William R. Thompson. 1989. "Long Cycles and Global War." In *Handbook of War Studies,* ed. Manus Midlarsky. Winchester, MA: Unwin Hyman.

Morrow, James D. Forthcoming. "Alliances and Asymmetry: An Alternative to the Capability Aggregation Model of Alliances." *American Journal of Political Science.*

Most, Benjamin A., Philip Schrodt, Randolph M. Siverson, and Harvey Starr. 1990. "Border and Alliance Effects in the Diffusion of Major Power Conflict, 1815–1965." In *Prisoners of War,* ed. Charles S. Gochman and Alan Ned Sabrosky. Lexington, MA: D. C. Heath.

Most, Benjamin A., and Harvey Starr. 1976. "Techniques for the Detection of Diffusion: Geopolitical Consideration in the Spread of War." Presented at the annual meeting of the International Studies Association, Toronto.

Most, Benjamin A., and Harvey Starr. 1980. "Diffusion, Reinforcement, Geo-politics and the Spread of War." *American Political Science Review* 74:932–46.

Most, Benjamin A., and Harvey Starr. 1981. "Theoretical and Methodological Issues in the Study of Diffusion and Contagion: Examples from the Research on War." Presented at the annual meeting of the International Studies Association, Philadelphia.

Most, Benjamin A., and Harvey Starr. 1983. "Conceptualizing 'War': Consequences for Theory and Research." *Journal of Conflict Resolution* 27:137–59.

Most, Benjamin A., and Harvey Starr. 1984. "International Relations Theory, Foreign Policy Substitutability, and 'Nice' Laws." *World Politics* 36:383–406.

Most, Benjamin A., and Harvey Starr. 1985. "Polarity, Preponderance, and Power Parity in the Generation of International Conflict. Presented at the annual meeting of the International Studies Association, Washington, DC.

Most, Benjamin A., and Harvey Starr. 1989. *Inquiry, Logic and International Politics.* Columbia, SC: University of South Carolina Press.

Most, Benjamin A., and Harvey Starr. 1990. "Theoretical and Logical Issues in the Study of International Diffusion." *Journal of Theoretical Politics* 2:391–412

Most, Benjamin A., Harvey Starr, and Randolph Siverson. 1989. "The Logic and Study of the Diffusion of International Conflict." In *Handbook of War Studies*, ed. Manus Midlarsky. Boston: Allen & Unwin.

Moyal, J. G. 1949. "Distribution of Wars in Time." *Journal of The Royal Statistical Society* 112:446–58.

Mueller, John. 1989. *Retreat from Doomsday: The Obsolescence of Major War.* New York: Henry Holt.

Naroll, Raoul. 1965. "Galton's Problem: The logic of Cross-Cultural Analysis." *Social Research* 32:428–51.

Olson, Mancur, and Richard Zeckhauser. 1966. "An Economic Theory of Alliances." *Review of Economics and Statistics* 46:266–79.

O'Loughlin, John. 1984. "Geographic Models of International Conflicts." In *Political Geography: Recent Advances and Future Directions,* ed. P. J. Taylor and J. House. London: Croom Helm.

O'Loughlin, John. 1986. "Spatial Models of International Conflicts: Extending Current Theories of War Behavior." *Annals of the Association of American Geographers* 76:63–80.

O'Loughlin, John. 1987. "The Contribution of Political Geography to the Study of International Conflicts: A Research Agenda." Presented at the annual meeting of the American Political Science Association, Chicago.

O'Loughlin, John, and Luc Anselin. 1990. "Bringing Geography Back to the Study of International Relations: Spatial Dependence and Regional Context in Africa, 1966–78. *International Interactions* 17:29–61.

O'Loughlin, John, and H. van der Wusten. 1986. "Geography, War and Peace: Notes for a Contribution to a Revived Political Geography." *Progress in Human Geography* 10:326–52.

Organski, A. F. K., and Jacek Kugler. 1980. *The War Ledger.* Chicago: University of Chicago Press.

Osterud, O. 1988. "The Uses and Abuses of Geopolitics." *Journal of Peace Research* 25:191–99.

O'Sullivan, P. 1986. *Geopolitics.* New York: St. Martin's Press.

Rand McNally. 1981. *Atlas of World History.* Chicago: Rand McNally.

Rapoport, Anatol. 1960. *Fights, Games, and Debates.* Ann Arbor: University of Michigan Press.

Rapoport, Anatol. 1966. "Two Views of Conflict: Cataclysmic and Strategic Models." *Proceedings of the International Peace Research Association Inaugural Conference.* Assen, Neth.: Van Gorcum.

Rasler, Karen A., and William R. Thompson. 1983. "Global Wars, Public Debts, and the Long Cycle." *World Politics* 35:489–516.

Richardson, Lewis F. 1960. *The Statistics of Deadly Quarrels*. Chicago: Quadrangle Books.

Riker, W. H. 1962. *The Theory of Political Coalitions*. New Haven: Yale University Press.

Rosenau, J. N. 1980. "The Adaptation of National Societies: A Theory of Political Behavior and Transformation." In *The Scientific Study of Foreign Policy*. Rev. ed. London: Frances Pinter.

Ross, Marc, and Elizabeth Homer. 1976. "Galton's Problem in Cross-National Research." *World Politics* 29:1–28.

Rummel, R. J. 1979. *Understanding Conflict and War: War, Power, Peace*. Beverly Hills: Sage.

Russett, B. 1963. "The Calculus of Deterrence." *Journal of Conflict Resolution* 7:97–109.

Sabrosky, Alan N. 1975. "The Utility of Interstate Alliances." Presented at the annual meeting of the International Studies Association, Washington, DC.

Sabrosky, Alan N. 1980. "Interstate Alliances: Their Reliability and the Expansion of War." In *The Correlates of War II: Testing Some Realpolitik Models*, ed. J. David Singer. New York: Free Press.

Schattschneider, E. E. 1960. *The Semi-Sovereign People: A Realist's View of Democracy in America*. New York: Holt, Rinehart and Winston.

Shepherd, William R. 1932. *Atlas of Modern History*. New York: Henry Holt.

Singer, J. David. 1974. "The Historical Experiment as a Research Strategy in the Study of World Politics." *Political Inquiry* 2:23–42.

Singer, J. David, Stuart A. Bremer, and John Stuckey. 1972. "Capability Distribution, Uncertainity, and Major Power War, 1820–1965." In *Peace, War, and Numbers*, ed. Bruce Russett. Beverly Hills: Sage.

Singer, J. David, and Melvin Small. 1968. "Alliance Aggregation and the Onset of War." In *Quantitative International Politics*, ed. J.D. Singer. New York: Free Press.

Singer, J. David, and Melvin Small. 1972. *The Wages of War, 1816–1965*. New York: Wiley.

Singer, J. David, and Melvin Small. 1974. "Foreign Policy Indicators: Predictors of War in History and in the State of the World Message." *Policy Sciences* 5:271–96.

Siverson, Randolph M. 1980. "War and Change within the International System." In *Change in the International System*, ed. O. R. Holsti, R. M. Siverson, and A. George. Boulder, CO: Westview.

Siverson, Randolph, and George Duncan. 1976. "Stochastic Models of International Alliance Initiation." In *Mathematical Models in International Relations*, ed. Dina Zinnes and John Gillespie. New York: Praeger.

Siverson, Randolph M., and Joel King. 1979. "Alliances and the Expansion of War." In *To Augur Well: Early Warning Indicators in World Politics*, ed. J. D. Singer and M. D. Wallace. Beverly Hills: Sage.

Siverson, Randolph M., and Joel King. 1980. "Attributes of National Alliance Membership and War Participation, 1815–1965." *American Journal of Political Science* 24:1–15.

Siverson, Randolph M., and Harvey Starr. 1988. "Alliance and Border Effects on the

War Behavior of States: Refining the Interaction Opportunity Model of Diffusion." Presented at the Third World Congress of the Peace Science Society (International), College Park, MD.

Siverson, Randolph M., and Harvey Starr. 1989. "Alliance and Border Effects on the War Behavior of States: Refining the Interaction Opportunity Model." *Conflict Management and Peace Science* 10:21–46.

Siverson, Randolph M., and Michael P. Sullivan. 1983. "The Distribution of Power and the Onset of War." *Journal of Conflict Resolution* 27:473–94.

Siverson, Randolph M., and Michael Sullivan. 1984. "Alliances and War: A New Examination of an Old Problem." *Conflict Management and Peace Science* 8:1–15.

Siverson, Randolph M., and Michael R. Tennefoss. 1984. "Power, Alliance and the Escalation of International Conflict, 1915–1965." *American Political Science Review* 78:1057–69.

Skjelsbaek, Kjell. 1971. "Shared Membership in Intergovernmental Organizations and Dyadic War, 1865–1964." In *The United Nations: Problems and Prospects*, ed. Edwin H. Fedder. St. Louis: Center for International Studies.

Sloan, G. R. 1988. *Geopolitics in United States Strategic Policy, 1890–1987*. New York: St. Martin's Press.

Small, Melvin, and J. David Singer. 1982. *Resort to Arms: International and Civil Wars, 1816–1980*. Beverly Hills: Sage.

Snyder, G. H., and P. Diesing. 1977. *Conflict among Nations*. Princeton, NJ: Princeton University Press.

Sorokin, P. A. 1937. *Social and Cultural Dynamics*. Vol. 3 of *Fluctuation of Social Relationships, War and Revolution*. New York: American Book Co.

Spillerman, S. 1970. "The Causes of Racial Disturbances: A Comparison of Alternative Explanations." *American Sociological Review* 35:627–49.

Sprout, H. 1963. "Geopolitical Hypotheses in Technological Perspective." *World Politics* 15:187–212.

Sprout, H., and M. Sprout. 1956. *Man-Milieu Relationship Hypotheses in the Context of International Politics*. Princeton, NJ: Princeton University Center of International Studies.

Sprout, H., and M. Sprout. 1965. *The Ecological Perspective on Human Affairs*. Princeton, NJ: Princeton University Press.

Sprout, H., and M. Sprout. 1969. "Environmental Factors in the Study of International Politics." In *International Politics and Foreign Policy*, ed. J. N. Rosenau. New York: Free Press.

Spykman, N. J. 1938. "Geography and Foreign Policy." *American Political Science Review* 32:28–50.

Starr, Harvey. 1972. *War Coalitions*. Lexington, MA: D. C. Heath.

Starr, Harvey. 1975. *Coalitions and Future Wars*. Beverly Hills: Sage.

Starr, Harvey. 1978a. "'Opportunity' and 'Willingness' as Ordering Concepts in the Study of War." *International Interactions* 4:363–87.

Starr, Harvey. 1978b. "Alliances: Tradition and Change in American Views on Foreign Military Entanglements." In *American Thinking about Peace and War*, ed. Ken Booth and Moorhead Wright. New York: Barnes & Noble.

Starr, Harvey. 1987. "Opportunity, Borders and the Diffusion of International Conflict: An Overview and Some Observations." Presented at the annual meeting of the American Political Science Association, Chicago.

Starr, Harvey. 1990. "Democratic Dominoes." Presented at a conference on "Democracy and Foreign Policy," University of California, Davis.

Starr, Harvey. 1991. "Joining Political and Geographic Perspectives: Geopolitics and International Relations." *International Interactions* 17:1–9.

Starr, Harvey, and B. A. Most. 1976. "The Substance and Study of Borders in International Relations Research." *International Studies Quarterly* 20:581–620.

Starr, Harvey, and B. A. Most. 1978. "A Return Journey: Richardson, 'Frontiers,' and Wars in the 1946–1965 Era." *Journal of Conflict Resolution* 22:441–67.

Starr, Harvey, and B. A. Most. 1983. "Contagion and Border Effects on Contemporary African Conflict." *Comparative Political Studies* 16:92–117.

Starr, Harvey, and B. A. Most. 1985. "The Forms and Processes of War Diffusion: Research Update on Contagion in African Conflict." *Comparative Political Studies* 18:206–27.

Stockholm International Peace Research Institute. 1970. *SIPRI Yearbook of World Armaments and Disarmament 1968/69*. New York: Humanities Press.

Stohl, Michael. 1980. "The Nexus of Civil and International Conflict." In *Handbook of Political Conflict*, ed. Ted Robert Gurr. New York: Free Press.

Sullivan, John D. 1974. "International Alliances." In *International Systems*, ed. Michael Haas. New York: Chandler.

Taylor, E. B. 1899. "On a Method of Investigating the Development of Institutions Applied to the Laws of Marriage and Descent." *Journal of the Royal Anthropological Institute* 18:245–72.

Tobler, W. 1979. "Cellular Geography." In *Philosophy in Geography*, ed. S. Gale and G. Olsson. Dordrecht: Reidel.

Tuchman, Barbara. 1962. *The Guns of August*. New York: Dell.

Tufte, Edward R. 1974. *Data Analysis for Politics and Policy*. Englewood Cliffs, NJ: Prentice Hall.

Velleman, P. F., and R. E. Welsch. 1981. "Efficient Computing of Regression Diagnostics," *American Statistician* 35:234–42.

Walt, S. M. 1985. "Alliance Formation and the Balance of Power." *International Security* 9:3–43.

Waltz, Kenneth. 1954. *Man, the State and War*. New York: Columbia University Press.

Waltz, Kenneth. 1979. *Theory of International Politics*. Reading, PA: Addison-Wesley.

Ward, Michael D. 1982. *Research Gaps in Alliance Dynamics*. Denver: University of Denver Monograph Series in World Affairs.

Ward, Michael D., and Andrew Kirby. 1987. "Reexamining Spatial Models of International Conflicts." *Annals of the Association of American Geographers* 77:279–83.

Wayman, Frank W. 1990. "Alliances and War: A Time-Series Analysis." In *Prisoners of War*, ed. Charles Gochman and Alan Ned Sabrosky. Lexington, MA: Lexington Books.

Weede, E. 1975a. *Weltpolitik und Kriegsursachen Im 20 Jahrhundert.* Munich: Oldenbourg.

Weede, E. 1975b. "World Order in the Fifties and Sixties: Dependence, Deterrence and Limited Peace. *Peace Science Society (International) Papers* 14:49–80.

Welsh, William A. 1984. "Inter-nation Interaction and Political Diffusion: Notes toward a Conceptual Framework." Presented at the annual meeting of the International Studies Association, Atlanta.

Wilkinson, David. 1980. *Deadly Quarrels.* Berkeley, CA: University of California Press.

Wright, Quincy. 1965. *A Study of War.* Rev. ed. Chicago: University of Chicago Press.

Yamamoto, Yoshinobu. 1990. "Rationality or Chance: The Expansion and Control of War." In *Prisoners of War,* ed. Charles S. Gochman and Alan Ned Sabrosky. Lexington, MA: D. C. Heath.

Yamamoto, Yoshinobu, and Stuart A. Bremer. 1980. "Wider Wars and Restless Nights: Major Power Intervention in Ongoing War." In *The Correlates of War II: Testing Some Realpolitik Models,* ed. J. D. Singer. New York: Free Press.

Zinnes, Dina. 1976a. *Contemporary Research in International Relations.* New York: Free Press.

Zinnes, Dina A. 1976b. "The Problem of Cumulation." In *In Search of Global Patterns,* ed. James N. Rosenau. New York: Free Press.

Zipf, G. K. 1949. *Human Behavior and the Principle of Least Effort.* Cambridge, MA: Addison-Wesley.

Index